WIN AT LIFE
And Positively Sparkle!

An Olympian's Advice for Success

To Valerie
All the best!
Barbara Berezowski

BARBARA BEREZOWSKI

Win at Life and Positively Sparkle! An Olympian's Advice for Success

ISBN: 9780991778409
eISBN: 9780991778416

Book cover designed by Rob Melvin: www.envisionarydesigns.com;
Book pages designed by Aaron Welch: bigadesigns.com;
Author photo by John Goldstein Photography: www.johngoldstein.net.

Barbara Berezowski is an Olympian on and off the ice. Her book, *Win At Life and Positively Sparkle! An Olympian's Advice For Success,* will inspire, enlighten, and coach you to be an Olympian in life!

-Scott Hamilton
1984 Olympic Gold Medalist

Barbara Berezowski was always dedicated, motivated and inspirational when she was Canadian Champion. Her book is a reflection of her spirit!

-Johnny Johns
Former US Pair & Dance Champion, World & Olympic Coach

In *Win At Life and Positively Sparkle,* Barbara shares all the powerful qualities that made her a World Professional Champion and Olympian. She doesn't just "talk the talk," she "walks the walk." This book tells you how to think like a champion—and live like a champion!

-Maxine Taylor
Georgia's First Licensed Astrologer

I have seen Barbara speak. I have seen her transform the energy in a room. The audience sits up. They listen and focus on her words. Afterwards with purpose, her audience walks and talks taller. She has the ability to motivate. Simply, this is Barbara. Having her wisdom, knowledge and strategies for empowering anyone in written form is a guide for bettering one's relationships internally, personally and professionally.

-Rick Mamros
RJ Mamros financial advisory Services

A true champion both on and off the ice, it's obvious that the powerful lessons Barbara learned from skating and from living life to its fullest have been shared with others through this book. The sheer joy that we saw in her skating, she expresses eloquently in writing to encourage everyone who reads it to pursue their own goals and dreams.

-Skate Canada

- DEDICATION -

I am dedicating this book to my beloved father, who I dearly miss. I have him to thank for teaching me the importance of love and devotion, for nurturing my spirit and showing me how to appreciate God's gift, life. He was goodness and gentleness personified. Gone but not forgotten; forever in my heart… Rest in peace, Dad. I love you.

~And~

To the special one, who inspires me to "Shine On" each and every day.

Barbara Berezowski and David Porter, Ice Follies 1980

- INTRODUCTION -

We are born into this world; it is a big marvelous place, full of wonder and opportunities. It doesn't matter who you are or where you come from, you have great potential and this world is just waiting for you to make your individual mark. Throughout your life, you contribute in various ways and it is done through your thoughts, your behavior and your actions. Each of us has our own path and it is the life experiences and social interactions along the way that shape us into who we become. It's an adventure for sure, one that many times includes unexpected twists and turns and a myriad of individual triumphs and tragedies. There are happy times and sad times and even with well laid out plans, things may not go as you had envisioned, but that is life, as they say. With the proper mindset, you will view these situations and events in life as the necessary lessons to be taken in order to develop and evolve into something bigger and stronger. Life experiences are indispensable. They are the tools to teach you how to survive and how to excel. We, as humans, are quite remarkable and extremely capable to endure and overcome.

So why then, do so many people struggle with low self-esteem? There are opportunities of greatness lost to them because they don't believe in themselves or in their potential. They dwell in a world of negativity, which doesn't help. Are you one of them?

If you look at this world as an unfair environment, where the rich get richer and you are here as a target for everyone to keep you down at the bottom of the ladder of success, this book is for you. Do you know of someone who wonders why everyone else seems to excel while all the bad things keep happening to them? Now is the time to end those negative thoughts.

So how do you STOP that toxic mindset? When you learn to effectively manage your thoughts and feelings, you stop the negativity; you become aware of the possibilities and opportunities around you. You become more aware of the boundless potential within you. You will become more successful in your personal and professional life. If you are a student and/or an athlete, your enthusiasm, drive and determination will improve. This enables you to begin the journey to your goal, and begin to enjoy life more. I WANT YOU to be in a happier place, become more productive, make more money or achieve your dreams.

In this book, I share my method of looking at life in a positive way. I would like you to consider the possibilities that await you when you change your outlook. I want you to be open-minded to this way of thinking. By doing so, you enable yourself to accept and embrace all the opportunities life has to offer. A positive attitude is essential to live your life full of enthusiasm, appreciation and a willingness to go after your dreams. I know, you're probably thinking that everyone and their brother, it seems, has written a book on positive thinking, so what makes this book different from the rest?

Simple. It's MY advice. As an Olympian, I have experienced the benefits of approaching everything in life with a positive attitude. I know the amount of dedication and determination one must have and the commitment one must make to go after and achieve a dream. A positive outlook in my life is one of the most important precursors to my achievements and this is the main focus of my message to you. I was a Canadian figure skating Champion. I competed at the 1976 Winter Olympic Games in Innsbruck, Austria and then went on to become a World Professional Figure Skating Champion.

I want to give you insight into how a champion thinks. I want you to have the confidence to succeed and a simple tweaking of how you look at life can do just that. Living your life with a positive outlook will make you sparkle inside and out and that I know is true. I am following my heart and sharing my excitement with you by putting my thoughts into the pages of this book because I know how wonderful living this way can be. I have had many successes and I am grateful for the opportunities I have had, but more importantly, I understand how precious life is and there is no greater reason to be grateful than that.

This book is a direct result of my personal passion for living each day with joy and sharing that joy with others. I look at this as an opportunity to reach out to you and offer what I have learned. For years, I have had this over-whelming urge to put my thoughts down on paper in order to inspire and empower others. I want to give back by teaching what I know and have you experience life in this way too. No matter what you desire, if you have the will to try, I encourage you to look at life from a different perspective. I purposely choose to live my life with happiness and I want you to do the same. Everyone has great potential and everyone deserves to be supported and encouraged. This is what I hope this book will help you realize.

I am here to encourage you, as a motivator. This is what I do with my clients as a personal development coach and it is what I do as a motivational speaker. Think of me as your personal coach and I will empower you. You will learn the importance of tapping into your positive energy and by doing so; you will begin looking at the world in a new light. My goal is to help you grow into all that you can be. I believe strongly that everyone should live their life in a positive way and it is their decision to live that way or not.

Being good, being kind and being positive is the message I deliver. There is a powerful source of positive energy within all of us and because I have an awareness of that, I consciously allow that energy to flow freely through me and apply it to whatever I am doing.

I realized early that I seemed to have a positive effect on people. I never sat myself down to try to figure out why, it was just a nice feeling and I went with it. I was just being me. Now, as an adult, I see that I have always lived my life this way. It has come to me in the most natural of ways. There have been many people that have mentored me along my path and I am grateful to have received their love, encouragement and teachings. I truly believe that I was put on this earth to receive and pass along these messages of motivation and to help others to be happy. Having a positive attitude towards life is the foundation of living a happy life.

It is not my intention to come across as some kind of mythical fairy sprinkling pixie dust over the world, magically making people walk around with perma-smiles on their faces. That happy image, where everything seems perfect in a sanitized world; where everyone has a perfect little family, lives in perfect little houses on perfect little streets, wearing their perfect little outfits and so on… is more like an opening scene of a Hollywood horror flick… and just as fake. Quite the contrary, life can be difficult at times and I have had my share of trials and tribulations, but I have always looked at the big picture and dealt with issues the best way I knew how. I am convinced that we all have a choice; to be positive and work through it, or not. Allowing my inner child to always shine through has always been one of my strongest positivity factors. Don't be afraid to be a grown up kid at times, let your guard down and just be. It is a quality you'll find in the most endearing people.

Have faith and be open to the possibilities and everything will find its place. How many times have you heard someone say, "Don't worry, it'll work out" but you didn't feel confident that it would? You most likely felt that way because you didn't believe that it would. With positivity, you look at that same statement in an entirely different way. I am here to encourage you to look at life and live in a positive way so that you can become a believer in the possibilities. It is not a unique or new concept. In fact over the years, it has been a subject visited and re-visited many times over, yet somehow the simplicity of the plan is still lost on so many.

If you find yourself in a place where you are hungry for change and you know in your heart that it is time to take on something new, then I congratulate you. This is progress and when you progress, you are accomplishing. Your achievements make you feel more alive. You need to act on these feelings.

Welcome everything with open arms. Be open to possibilities. Life is wonderful and there are so many doors to open and windows to peek through. Why not do more than that? Be brave and adventurous and take a step outside. When you apply the positivity factor to live your life, your mind, body and spirit will be in synchronicity with one another and this will make you more open to exploring something new. You will have harmony and be at peace. Imagine all the adventures that lay ahead. How exciting!

In This Book, You Will Learn:

- How to overcome your obstacles and be the best you can be.
- How to be more accepting of goodness and experience life in a happier way.
- Why positivity is so good for you and what it can help you accomplish.
- How to live with your life with a purpose and recognize a world of opportunities.

When you get a handle on thinking positively, your life WILL change—and the "Why Me" whining will become a thing of the past. Are you ready to stop blaming everyone else for keeping you down? Are you ready to take on the responsibility to start living more positively?

Be passionate. Love life. Believe in yourself. It's time! With a positive attitude, you will *Win at Life and Positively Sparkle!*

- CONTENTS -

SPARKLE
BE MOTIVATED

- CHAPTER ONE -

SOUL SEARCHING TIME

"Cherish your visions and dreams, as they are the children of your soul; the blueprints of your ultimate achievements."
Napoleon Hill

All things are possible when you have inner peace. Everything in this world is part of an energy field and there is a human energy within us. This energy force within us, is shared when we connect and interact with others every day. Once you are able to tap into your own energy force, you will become more aware of who you are as an individual and realize that you are capable of many wonderful things. My desire is to inspire you to live a life with a positive attitude. Be motivated to look at life and appreciate it for all it is and for all it can be.

I want to raise your awareness and empower you to not only look at life in a positive light but to also realize that you must take responsibility for this power. You choose how to deal with issues, no one else. Make the choice to rejoice. It is imperative for your well-being, and for the well-being of those around you; to honestly and openly appreciate everything life has to offer.

You may feel a little hesitant in accepting this theory, perhaps feeling that it has no relevance when dealing with your individual situation. You may be thinking that it is easy to give the rah-rah speech when you are on the winning side but how pertinent is it when you are in a situation that is challenging? Well, even if you're on the losing side of the game, you must believe in yourself and know that there is always a way to overcome any obstacle. I would like to give you the motivation to look at life differently. You must be committed to yourself and to your own happiness.

I have recently become very interested in the positive psychology movement. There is an increasing interest in researching and analyzing the benefits of having a sunny disposition and although it is realized that not everyone is born with it, the experts agree that we can all learn how to bring more meaning and satisfaction into our lives.

Everything matters in life. Religion teaches you this. You are to be accepting of the good, the bad, the happy and the sad. People are different and it must be this way for us to understand that this is what makes us who we are. People matter because how you interact with others is what makes life worth living. Throughout life you learn to deal with different situations and you develop social skills. Problems and upsets are important, whether you like them or not, because it builds your character and strengthens your faith. When you have meaning and purpose in your life, you are well on your way to a state of well-being and with that, happiness.

Happiness, for some of you is a constant state and is as natural as breathing but for others it is more of a challenge. People who are satisfied with life eventually have even more reason to be satisfied, because happiness leads to desirable outcomes in sports, at school and at work. Happiness leads to positive results when interacting with others socially and even to good health and long life. The good life is hard work, and there are no shortcuts to sustained happiness.

It is so important to believe in yourself and have the desire to try anything you wish to. I want my advice to push you to grow and become better. Why not? You are wonderful. You have talent. You have experience. You are unique. You are worth it. When I hear my clients say, "Oh, I haven't done much" or "no one would believe I can do it," or "I'm just..." I simply say "STOP!" Never say that you are "just a cook," "just a clerk," "just a driver." Successful people believe in themselves. Have you ever heard someone say: "I'm just a Doctor"? No matter who you are or what you do, hold your head up and be proud. You are an essential piece of the puzzle when we look at the human race. You are as important to the fabric of life as anyone else is.

> Happiness leads to positive results when interacting with others socially and even to good health and long life.

Think back to all the things that you have experienced to date. Think of all your accomplishments and disappointments, big and small. These are the things that have helped shape and develop you into who you are. There are lessons in all those memories. Take that valuable data, analyze it, work with it, develop a plan and you will be surprised at the treasure trove of information you will have. You can use this to build on your strengths and improve on your weaknesses.

I have had the good fortune to realize my dream of participating in the Olympics. I have spent my life striving to do my best, not just in athletics but in life in general. As a person, I am at peace knowing that I live my life to the best of my ability. I live my life consciously incorporating love, kindness, honesty, compassion, humor and sincerity into my daily activities. I care about and respect myself but it is also important for me to care about and respect others. It is how I choose to be and I do it the best way I can. I know you've heard people speak about their personal journeys, but listen carefully. The terms, "be the best" or "be your best" are quite different. You can strive to be the best there is; or do something to the best of your ability. It all depends on your belief system. You choose what's important to you and how to apply yourself. In my heart, I believe it is far better to "always do your best." I believe there is a deeper sense of gratification when you know you've done your best at the end of the day. With determination and self-confidence, you will be successful.

There are many opportunities in life and you should grab and hold on to as many as you can. Be adventurous, be confident; never be afraid to try. Now, I'm not saying to go cliff diving or anything like that (unless that's your passion); what I'm saying is: don't deny yourself something wonderful that could be life changing for you because you are afraid to fail. Just give it your best shot and be honest with yourself. This practice has served me well and I really am quite appreciative for all the learning experiences. I am extremely thankful for all the successes and gifts in my life. I have learned from so many wonderful teachers and in an effort to pay-it-forward, I'd like to share what I have learned with you.

I believe what gives me the credibility to offer my knowledge to you is my list of accomplishments and experiences. Throughout my personal journey to the Olympics, I knew first hand, that the number one factor to achieve success is that you must believe in yourself. My life has been an ever-changing adventure and it has led me down a multitude of different roads, not all of which were smooth and freshly paved. I have climbed some of the highest mountains and found myself in the deepest of valleys as well.

I say this in a figurative sense, although I did travel this great, big, beautiful world and have seen some amazing sights. The point I am trying to make here is, I feel blessed that I have. This is what life is all about and we need to accept it and be prepared for whatever may come our way. In order for you to understand why I am so passionate about my message of tapping into your positive energy to live life to the fullest, I want to share some of my story with you.

Back to the Beginning

As a young girl, I found great inspiration in the skating champions of the day. I saw something in them I admired. I saw confidence, a self-assurance that was difficult to hide. Even at an early age, mostly because of how I was raised, I believed that anything was possible if you worked hard and believed in yourself. In my mind, I put myself into their shoes, (or I should say skates), I set my first goal, I envisioned myself as a champion.

Like many other children growing up in Canada, being able to ice skate was a must amongst your peers. Everyone seemed to be able to skate and it looked like so much fun because it was such a social activity as well. Canada's figure skating Superstar was Barbara Ann Scott. Even though she was the 1948 Olympic Champion, she has always been a huge sports celebrity in Canada. I admired her beauty and grace. For many years, it was commonplace for young girls to ask for a Barbara Ann Scott doll to appear under the Christmas Tree. It wasn't difficult to decide that this was a sport for me. Besides, in my seven-year-old mind, I believed it was justified that I take up skating because after all, like Barbara Ann Scott, I was a CANADIAN GIRL and my name was BARBARA! Did there need to be another reason?!

My parents loved skating too, especially my Dad. He would tell me stories of when he was a young boy back in Poland; as soon as the local pond would freeze over, he would grab his skates and spend countless hours out there just enjoying the sensation of speed and the freedom he felt while gliding on ice. My German mother's childhood sport was swimming but she loved watching skating as well so sports was considered a great activity in our family. It wasn't a hard sell to convince them to put me into skating and from that point onward, I became a serious skater and joined a figure skating club that was affiliated with the CFSA (Canadian Figure Skating Association). I diligently learned the basics, practiced for hours on end and eventually began to compete. I skated as a "ladies single skater" and was pretty good until a growth spurt sent my co-ordination out of the window, never to return. I was graceful and expressive but my jumping skills were not up to par and realistically, I knew that there was no hope of challenging anyone in competition, looking like a spider with skates on.

My real love was ice dancing though and I was so good at it. In fact, I passed all the testing there was, all the way to the Gold level, by the age of fourteen. As I said, I was too tall and lanky to be a good single skater (with all the jumps and spins) but my height was a bonus for the elegant, elongated lines of ice dancing. The challenge in becoming a competitive ice dancer was finding a skating partner. The difficulty was always the ratio of females to males in figure skating. I don't know what the exact numbers were but suffice it to say, there were many more females then males in the skating rinks across the country. Remember, this is Canada and boys and hockey go together like peanut-butter and jam.

Even though the odds were not in my favor, I always held out hope that one day I would find a skating partner. "If it was meant to be, it would happen."

It was meant to be. In the summer of my fifteenth year, the doorway to the possibility of finding a skating partner opened up wide for me. The Canadian Ice Dance Champions at the time were Mary Church and David Sutton. As fate would have it, they practiced at two different arenas in the Toronto area. They were instrumental in arranging for me, at one rink, to try out with a male ice dancer they knew, at another. We skated once together and it was decided that we were a good match so we began our career together under the tutelage of our first coaches, Margaret and Bruce Hyland. I now had a partner and his name was David Porter. I changed disciplines and devoted my life to ice dancing 100% that day. Putting two skaters together and working through the new feeling of having someone else's feet in such close proximity to you was a challenge for me. There were many tumbles and along with it bumps and bruises. So many that we were lovingly nicknamed Crash and Crumble but we eventually got it right. Marg and Bruce had wonderful spirit and worked very hard to get us to the point where we could enter a National Championship only six months later.

We were entered into the Junior Ice Dance category to make our debut on the national stage. I was in such awe of everything and everyone around me that I didn't get a chance to be nervous. It was an exhilarating whirlwind of a dream coming into focus for me. Before I knew it, I found myself standing in the middle of an ice surface in a building that housed thousands of spectators. We believed in our potential, we were trained and properly prepared but we were there only to introduce ourselves and show our stuff. There was no pressure to win because we were not expected to. By the end of the event, we were the Junior Champions of Canada in Ice Dance! What? My head was spinning. It had only been six months since my door of opportunity opened and David and I had our first skate together. Wow! It all happened so quickly and everyone was so was shocked. I got a taste of success and I wanted more. I was now more committed than ever to work towards the next level of competition. I knew that as we progressed and moved up into the senior ranks of elite competition, the pressures would also intensify but that didn't scare me, I was hungry for more.

I must share all the skating accolades with David because as a dance team, there would always be the two of us out there on the ice. Without each other, none of this would have happened. I want to also make special mention of the many skating coaches and choreographers along the way. It is all such a team effort. When you see a Nascar racer take the checkered flag, it's not just the driver that wins the race. It's the family, the pit crew, the crew chief, the team owner, the sponsors that all have an important part in the success. In our case, it was the same; our parents, our coaches, our judges, executives and officials of the Canadian Figure Skating Association (now Skate Canada) that guided and helped shape us into the Champions and Olympians we became. It was a real team effort.

We have a very good program in Canada and the United States when it comes to our respective Skating Associations. Over the years, the executive and staff of both organizations under the umbrella of the ISU (International Skating Union) have worked and developed the best structure to ensure that every skater in the country is offered the best experience. Skate Canada as the governing body for figure skating in Canada has done an outstanding job to develop and promote our sport. Skating coaches around the world must be commended for their work as well. They all have passion for our sport and they are dedicated to their students. They put in many hours standing out there in the cold, often times extremely early in the morning, and they patiently guide and teach and train their skaters. What you may not realize is these skating coaches devote much of their off ice life to creating programs, selecting music and designing costumes as well. Figure skating coaches are extremely creative artists in their own right, many were champions themselves. They are skilled as instructors and advisors and therapists and have the patience of saints. The general public only sees them on TV when the competitions take place, standing at the edge of the ice surface offering a very few words. They anxiously watch their students perform and then await their arrival into the "kiss and cry" area at the end of the rink to receive their marks. Believe me; they go through a great deal of emotional stress as well. They are to be appreciated and respected for their achievements.

The most influential of my coaches was Marijane Stong. She, along with her husband, Louis Stong, were the highly successful team that developed many of Canada's National, World and Olympic Champions of skating. They are both well-deserved Honoured Members of the Skate Canada Hall of Fame for their contributions to Canadian figure skating. I am so proud of Marijane and Louis and happy that they have been recognized for their great achievements. With Marijane's guidance throughout the years, there were many competitions, many ups and downs and many tests of strength and courage for us. After all the many hours, days, weeks, months and years of hard work, injuries and sacrifices, recognition finally came. Winning numerous titles led to the exuberance of becoming Canadian National Champions, World Team Members and Olympians. She taught me so much, not just with the on-ice technique, but it was through her vision and guidance that I learned so much about how to handle life. She also sent us to Wilmington, Delaware in the USA each summer, to work with one of the top US coaches, Ron Ludington and train alongside the US Champions. We formed a close bond with the American skaters, and we learned so much from the ice dance greats: Judy Schwomeyer and James Sladky and Johnny Johns and Mary Karen Campbell.

While in the US, we entered the Summer Ice Dance competition, which still is an annual event, in beautiful Lake Placid, New York. We won that competition becoming the Lake Placid Summer Ice Dance Champions and began making our mark and becoming recognized in the USA. Marijane had the wisdom to know that you only get better when you train along with skaters that can challenge you. Each practice session becomes a mini competition and you are constantly striving to be the best. This makes you work harder each time out and you cannot help but improve. She was so much more than just my coach. Marijane was and is my friend, my idol and my mentor. I was groomed by the best. I owe so much to her and will be forever grateful.

It is difficult to describe the overwhelming pride I felt when I finally reached the top of that podium and was introduced as the Champion of Canada in Ice Dance. That was in 1975 and 1976, and the Men's Champion was Toller Cranston; the Ladies' Champion was Lynn Nightingale, and the Pair Champions were Candace Jones and Donald Fraser. Together, along with other extremely talented skaters that placed in the top three of Canada, we became Members of the World Figure Skating Team, representing Canada and with that, many trips across North America and Europe. Representing my country at world-class events was extremely exciting but nothing compared to the ultimate goal for any athlete… being named as a Member of the Olympic Team. Putting on that red Canadian Olympic uniform for the first time was an experience beyond comprehension. I will forever have the title of Olympian and that is something I will cherish for a lifetime.

The sport of Ice Dancing was included in the Winter Olympics for the first time in 1976 and those Games were held in the beautiful Tyrolean city of Innsbruck, Austria. The Austrian people of Innsbruck were so kind and welcoming, they were the perfect host. The experience of competing in an Olympic Games was overwhelming. To be a participant in a venue where all of the world's best athletes gather to compete is mind boggling. We spent our skating life meeting up with skaters from all over the world at the various skating competitions we attended. It becomes somewhat of a familiar environment because year after year, we would see the same people. At the Olympics, there were not just those known skating people, but many new types of athletes attending. Hockey players, skiers, bobsledders, speed skaters, ski jumpers, etc., all sharing the same experience. It is a much larger world stage and it is much more intense. The excitement and pressure levels are through the roof but then, so is the experience.

1976 Winter Olympics, Innsbruck, Austria

In Innsbruck, just outside the main arena, there was an outdoor speed skating oval that had an inner ice surface to be used as practice ice for figure skaters. It was surrounded by hundreds of flagpoles waving the official Olympic flags along with the flags of all the participating countries. Beyond that, in the distance, the entire town of Innsbruck was surrounded by the breathtakingly beautiful snow covered mountains that reached a height of more than 2,000 m above sea level. The

Opening Ceremonies: 1976 Winter Olympics, Innsbruck, Austria

highest mountain is the Bikkarspitze and it reaches a height of 2,749 m above sea level. It was a sight to behold, especially on one particular sun-drenched day in February 1976. Spectacular is the only word to describe it.

We found ourselves practicing our craft on that ice surface, within that speed skating oval… OUTSIDE! It was freezing but the sun was warm as it brilliantly shone down on Innsbruck. What an experience! It was like a scene out of the earlier Olympic Games that magically came across our black and white television screen in my living room as a child. The image took me back to the days when all of the skating events took place on frozen ice pads outdoors. There were no mighty stadiums built to host the events. We were modern day skaters and not accustomed to performing on any ice other than within a building with seating for at least 20,000 spectators. We found skating out in the elements a very foreign concept. Skating your program with sunglasses on and trying to be graceful while fighting against the wind was quite something. It reminded me of the images of Barbara Ann Scott winning the Olympics in 1948. I felt like I had boarded a time travel machine somehow and arrived in old-time Innsbruck. It was surreal, it was outstanding. It was an experience of a lifetime and it is one that I am so grateful for and will never forget.

In this 1976 Olympics, with Ice Dancing as a new event, we drew #1 in the skating order so we became the first dancers to take the ice. This made us an item for the record books; we had become the first skaters in the world to officially compete in an Olympic ice dance event.

Shortly after the Olympics in Innsbruck, Austria and the World Championships in Sweden in 1976, we were offered three contracts to turn professional. (Unlike today with many wealthy professionals competing in the Olympics, athletes had to be true amateurs to compete in the Olympics. In fact, if any athlete, whatever the sport, accepted one penny as payment for either performance or endorsements, they would lose their amateur status and be disqualified from competing.) We were given the option of turning professional and joining one of three professional skating shows. I was only 21 and could have competed for a few more years with sights set on a second Olympics however, realistically, we knew it would be too difficult to continue financially. Even though the Canadian government was beginning to help out athletes with some funding, it wasn't nearly enough to cover the expenses of 4 more years of training and so we decided it was time and we had to go pro.

In 1976, there were two well-established travelling ice skating shows, rich in tradition with distinguished reputations. These two shows were "Ice Capades" and Shipstads and Johnson's 'Ice Follies." The third offer came from the newly created "Stars On Ice" which would feature Toller Cranston and present a cast of champions. We took a leap of faith and signed a contract with Stars On Ice. Even though I had wanted to be a part of Ice Follies since childhood, I agreed to give Toller's "Stars On Ice" a try. It was a new concept, an evening of Champion skaters only, no glamorous stage sets and beautifully clad showgirls. The show's cast consisted of Canadian and American Figure Skating Champions and we did it all… we were the soloists, the pair teams, the group ensembles and such.

In hindsight, I guess we were onto something great because today, other than Disney's characters on ice, it is the only ice show concept featuring Champions that still exists. The days of the big Hollywood extravaganzas on ice (Ice Follies and Ice Capades) have gone the way of the Dodo bird. Our troop played smaller, more intimate venues across North America and we were competing against the big boys of show business. As I was in a partnership (with David) we had to mutually agree on any decision regarding our career and which contract we were going to sign. I agreed to give Stars On Ice a try but only if David promised to go with me to skate in Ice Follies, should the opportunity ever arise.

I certainly don't regret my decision because I had a wonderful time travelling with Stars On Ice. Even though there were some extremely challenging situations, there were also some over-the-top experiences as well. Toller Cranston was a Canadian Champion and a 1976 Olympic Bronze medalist who had a huge following, worldwide. His fans recognized his contribution to our sport because he introduced and incorporated a more artistic style that changed men's figure skating. In my opinion, it was a travesty that Toller Cranston was never awarded the marks allowing him to become world champion. He definitely deserved the title but back then, it was difficult to get past the Eastern European judges from ganging together to have their skaters reach the top. Yes, I am saying that deals were constantly being made in a dishonest way. Many of us were victims of that practice. Manipulation of the results did happen and even though it was all hushed for years, the skaters

1976 Canadian Winter Olympic Skating Team

were all aware of it. I was happy to see all that come out at the 2002 Salt Lake City Olympics when our Canadians Jamie Sale and David Pelletier were awarded the gold medal in Pairs, after the judging scandal was exposed. Biased judging wasn't unique to that event alone nor did it happen only at those Olympics. Thankfully, as a result of the media attention, the International Skating Union has implemented a new judging system to even out the playing field.

I enjoyed my time touring professionally with Toller in Stars On Ice. His personality was just as flamboyant as his style and it was always a trip to spend time with him. I admired Toller for his artistry and for his humor and intellect. I met so many wonderful people in our travels and the entire company, of cast and crew, became quite close. Some of the not so good times were the one or two night stands, travelling on buses and arriving only in time to start the show without a proper warm up or practice session. Our troop went through about three different owners of the show and with that, many rubber pay cheques that bounced all the way home. We found ourselves unemployed more than once but luckily, only long enough for the powers-to-be to find new investors just in time for the next performance to start. It was an unsettling time, leaving us bewildered and to some degree, disappointed that we had chosen this new concept show over the well established productions. It wasn't all good but it wasn't all bad either. The better times included meeting various foreign dignitaries, Heads of State, Royalty and Hollywood celebrities. We even got to perform on stage On Broadway at the iconic Palace Theatre in New York City.

Above all else, I always found my greatest satisfaction in signing autographs for the children along the way. Being an inspiration to others has always been important to me, mostly because of the Champions that came before me. Their behavior had an impact on my life. I remember being one of those children waiting for a celebrity's autograph. How wonderful I felt when I was acknowledged, after standing there with my pen and paper, hoping for the chance to meet them. Some of these North American skating legends were Mens Champions: Don Jackson, Richard Button, Jay Humphry, Donald Knight; Ladies Champions: Barbara Ann Scott, Carol Heiss, Peggy Fleming, Wendy Griner, Petra Burka, Karen Magnussen, Janet Lynn; Pairs Champions: Frances Dafoe and Norris Bowden, Barbara Wagner and Bob Paul, Maria and Otto Jelinek, Debbi Wilkes and Guy Revell, JoJo Starbuck and Kenneth Shelley, and Dance Champions: Paulette Doan and Kenneth Ormsby, Carole Forrest and Kevin Lethbridge, Donna Taylor and Bruce Lennie and Mary Church and David Sutton, just to name a few. They all took the time to give a kid some inspiration and it meant a lot to me. Their words of encouragement did not fall on deaf ears. I made it my mission, early on, to do the same when I grew up.

I would make time to sign autographs and converse with my fans if I ever achieved my dream of becoming a champion.

Even out of the limelight, no matter what the situation, a smile, a warm greeting, a wave, should never be too much for people to share. After all, it is good karma and it is the right thing to do.

My life in the sporting world led me to the glamour and excitement of becoming a performer in the entertainment industry. One experience always led to another. My life was never dull because there was always another adventure just around the corner and I looked forward to it with great anticipation.

We had believed that our days of competition were over when we left the amateur world of figure skating for the sequins and spotlights of show business, however that was not to be the case. Out of the blue, we received an invitation from the event organizers in Spain to compete in the World Professional Figure Skating Championships. Here was another of life's unexpected opportunities and we decided to accept it and proceeded to go back into training mode to prepare for the challenge. It was a pleasant surprise when we discovered that many of the international skating champions we had competed against in the Olympics were there (in Spain) as well. Seeing all the familiar faces made the event a bit of a reunion and it was a comfortable environment for us to return to. Our competitors now were professionals as well but it seemed that the clock had been turned back just a bit and everything was as it was in our amateur days. There was a great sense of accomplishment when we won the title of World Professional Ice Dance Champions because we had now beaten some of the same skaters that placed ahead of us in the Olympics. Away from the amateur judging games, we were finally recognized and awarded for what we actually did out there on the ice.

It was incredible to live the life of a sports celebrity. We went on to perform all over the world for another six years and… yes; I did eventually realize my dream of skating in the famous "Ice Follies" (which was every bit as wonderful as I imagined it to be). I am a firm believer in things happening for a reason and the saying "if it's meant to be, it will happen." We signed our contract with Ice Follies as the World Professional Champions and I felt I had finally found my way home. My dream and vision as a young girl was coming true and I was overjoyed. Everything seemed bigger than life to me, the arenas, the lights, the stage sets, the countless numbers of trucks to carry our costumes and props and equipment. It was overwhelming to arrive on my first day, something like a first day of high school, a little scared of the unknown, yet very excited at the proposition of a fantastic adventure. Lucky for me, there was Ann and Paul, two skaters that I knew from back home and they graciously welcomed me and took me under their wing to guide me along and help me feel at home. To this day, we are still so close and the friendship that I have with them is something that I cherish. The number of cast members of Ice Follies was large, the crew was made up of many and yet we all travelled together criss-crossing across North America like a tight knit family in a station wagon. It left me with many fond memories; too many to go into, it would take another book.

> I firmly believe in the importance of preparation for whatever the task might be.

I also had the chance to perform in a skating show in Seoul, South Korea for six months. Going to the Far East was something I had never anticipated but it was another road to take for me and I was always open to exploration. It was the other side of the world and it was a fantastic experience taking in the culture and the discoveries of what we found on a daily basis. I developed many friendships over the years but in all my travels around the world, none were as close as the bond that was formed between an American skating Champion, Leigh Ann and I. We were both adventurous souls and everyday was spent exploring. We spent our time in Korea making the most of every minute. We took in all the sights and sounds and experienced as much as humanly possible. We had built a strong foundation for a life-long friendship.

All good things come to pass and eventually, after 21 years of skating, I decided it was time to call it a day. It was time to move on to life-after-skating and so after our last show in South Korea, my life would evolve into another wonderful escapade. I returned home, retired from skating and put my well-travelled suitcases into storage. I was very excited to actually hang my clothes in a closet for longer than a week. I certainly saw my share of hotel rooms over the years so staying in one place was a luxury by this point.

Although I loved the experiences and all of the traveling, I had come to the realization that now I was ready to start a new chapter in life. It was time to hang up my skates. I taught skating in Nevada and California for a few years, had a wonderful time living in the sunshine and amongst the palm trees but I missed my family and decided to come back home to Canada. Retiring from skating (at 28) was difficult because it was a huge life transition for me. What do I do now? Who am I if not a skater?

The one thing that gets me from point to point is the fact that I am an eternal optimist. I always know that whatever route I take, there will be, at some point, the right path to follow and everything will play out as it is meant to.

To my surprise, even though it was now life after skating for me, more travel was in the cards when I took a position at a company in Toronto. It was fun and exhilarating to be globe-trotting again but this time wearing a different hat. No ice rinks in sight. A few years later, I met my future husband; after we married, we were blessed with the arrival of two wonderful sons. Life was grand and I was grateful. Motherhood for me is the best of what life has to offer. Over the years, as you watch your children grow, you come to realize what a gift life is.

I firmly believe in the importance of preparation for whatever the task might be. My life as an athlete taught me to always be prepared and to understand my challenges. I always felt strong, both mentally and physically and I felt invincible, even when I had to face trying circumstances.

So now, away from the spotlight and the arenas filled with thousands of spectators and with both feet planted firmly on the ground, I never imagined my strength would be tested again. Little did I know, I was about to come face to face with the biggest challenge of my life. It happened one week into the new millennium. That morning, in early 2000, when most people were still reveling in the millennium celebrations, my world was rocked with the most devastating situation that I ever had to face.

It started out as a great Saturday, early morning hockey games and goals scored by both sons had us all cheering and celebrating while cuddling up to our hot chocolates. The day was turning out to be a wonderful one and after a celebratory breakfast for the early morning goals, my husband left to go shopping, our youngest son left for a sleep-over and my other son and I remained home. Nothing out of the ordinary, just one of those great "family" weekends filled with good quality family time.

A few hours later, everything changed in an instant. We got the news that my husband wasn't coming home. He had suddenly passed away of a heart attack. He was only 41 and our children were only 9 and 10 years old at the time. Our lives, as we knew it, suddenly changed.

It was devastating. After the shock of it all, my mind was never at rest because there were so many questions in my head. "How would I now handle life, taking on both roles of a mother and father?" "How would I ensure that I would provide all the emotional strength necessary to help my children through this very traumatic event, when I was so devastated?" "How were we going to manage?" "What do I do and what do I say and how do I now handle life with everything resting on my shoulders alone?" I never really stopped to appreciate the difficult life of a single parent until those first few hours after I got the news and the reality of it all began to slowly sink in. I'd now have to be everything to my children, and they had to now accept a different life, one without their Dad.

These were the thoughts in my head and in my heart. I felt lost. All of my life's training as an elite athlete, both mentally and physically did not prepare me for this. Or did it?

Looking back at all that now, I have to say that my training as an athlete, as well as my strong family values and my positive outlook on life, were the tools that helped me through it all. I was so grateful for my Dad's love and emotional support and for the compassion of my wonderful friends who were there for me immediately. They all helped me through so much but at the end of the day, it was up to me to choose how I was going to handle everything. I know, in my heart, that it was being true to myself that helped get me through it all.

I have always cherished and nurtured my positive energy. I have guarded it with a strict conviction and oath to never allow anyone to tamper with it. I had the perseverance and tenacity to stay focused on my goals and I always believed in myself. This is what guided me through the deepest valley and back up the mountain. It took me a while but I eventually did it. I share all this with you to help you understand that I truly believe in the message I am sharing with you. If I can empower you to believe that you can win at life and to teach you to nurture your positive energy, you will flourish and shine.

You will find that being positive is magnetic. When you begin to look at things with a positive outlook and apply yourself in positive manner, you will attract positive results. My mission is to enlighten and inspire you. As I said earlier, even though we have no control over what comes our way, we do have the ability to choose how we deal with it.

This is what life is all about and we need to accept it and be prepared to adapt to whatever may come our way. When we are tired, we sleep. When we are hungry, we eat. It's basic instinct. When life gets tough, we must deal with it. Don't get me wrong, it is not an easy task but with focus, drive, determination and a strong belief system, you will get through it.

So what do I say? After the shock and after the grief, pull yourself together and move on. Forget the pity party, it serves no purpose and it is so detrimental to good health, yours and those around you. There is always a way and it is your decision to make. Have faith and believe in yourself.

Positive Energy Gives You a Positive Attitude

You are a positive person. If you stop and think about it, you will realize that you have had positive thoughts all your life but you are probably so focused on all the heavy things in life, you've just lost sight of that. Many times, people are so bogged down by the serious, mundane chores, duties, stresses and responsibilities in an adult life; they don't even realize they're walking around with tunnel vision, only seeing the problems facing them. This is where negative thoughts, feelings and emotions can take over and cloud your thinking.

Unlike most adults, children have that natural positive sparkle about them. Ever notice that sparkle in their eyes? They see life and all of its adventures as something wonderful and exciting. They can't help but look at everything in a positive light. It's as natural as breathing to them. They don't think about being positive, they just are. We were all children once, were we not? We were all like that. Remember how much fun it was to just run and jump into a puddle, or dance in the rain or jump into a huge pile of leaves? It was just purely for the fun of it.

So what happened? Who ever said that when you become an adult, you have to switch off the fun? Obviously, you mature as you age but where is it written that you can't feel joy for the simple things in life just because you enter adulthood? So be at peace, stop the worry and find that inner child.

The best way to deal with tough times is to tap into your inner positive energy for strength.

Dr. Deepak Chopra, the mind, body and spirit expert, identifies this as Self Power. He explains it as your immeasurable potential, your perfection, independent of the good and bad opinions of the world, which is totally fearless, it feels beneath no one or superior to no one. By getting in touch with this part of yourself, you will unfold or unlock all your potential. This is what I have been in tune with all my life. My positive outlook is my self-power.

Life is a gift and it is so beneficial to remind yourself of this everyday. With a positive outlook, issues and obstacles become manageable because once you are self-empowered, you have the tools to take on any task and you truly have the strength to keep moving forward. I am someone that has always felt that anything is possible. Even at a young age, I realized how precious life was and it's mostly because I have always allowed that inner child in me to shine through. I have my Dad to thank for that, he led by example and taught me so much about goodness and kindness and appreciation for the simple things. His inner child was always present, even up until the day he passed on at almost 93. I have discovered that the most endearing people have that quality.

You should love life and look at things in a positive way, always. This practice will brighten your outlook on life and as a result, you will appreciate living all the more. My wonderful parents taught me to be receptive to the opportunities that life has to offer. They always encouraged me to be open to the possibilities. They learned some very valuable lessons living through the incredibly difficult years of World War II. It was through their hardships, that they learned to value life. Even having gone through those trying times, they still remained true to their core values. It was through their incredible stories of survival that I learned that life is a gift to be cherished and that we should never take anything for granted. They understood the seriousness of life but they weren't afraid to let the "kid inside" come out to play. We all have that inner child in us, it is our spirit and it should never be suppressed. Always be open to that next adventure.

New Beginnings

Everyone is so enthusiastic and energized when the calendar reads January 1st every year. It's a new beginning, a chance to set off in a new direction, a chance to improve, a chance to start over. There is inspiration in just that, the thought that there is an opportunity available to us, each and every year. Happy New Year is a greeting and a chant that can be heard around the world and it is always uplifting because everyone knows that there are endless possibilities ahead. They are the chances to change, to improve, to become healthier, to take action and to start over.

A new year is a new beginning. It's a chance to forgive yourself for the projects that you did not complete, or the workout plan that you gave up on midway through the previous year, or the financial plan to get yourself out of debt that you sort of side-stepped. Don't focus on that, don't waste your energy worrying about why you didn't accomplish what you set out to do the previous year. That was last year. Adios! Say goodbye to those negative feelings and start anew.

With every new day, you are looking at a new beginning. It doesn't have to be the "New Year" to start. Think of it as a blank page, a clean, crisp sheet of paper that is of the finest quality and as white as snow. You hold the pen and own the creations that your imagination and efforts will bring. All the thoughts, feelings and actions throughout your life will go into creating your masterpiece. Whether you are an athlete aiming to be in the Olympics, a student studying to earn a scholarship, or a entrepreneur setting off on a dream to have your business ranked in Fortune 500 one day, you must have passion and purpose and be dedicated and driven to follow through.

10 Sparkle Tips

1. Forgive yourself and forget about your disappointments. Time to get rid of that clutter and all those memories you have in your head of everything that you perceive as a negative experience in your life. They are all learning experiences.

2. Clear your mind, cleanse your system, just like a car, regular tune-ups are a good practice. Don't be a hoarder of needless regrets. It is never too late. You can start now. In order to move forward, you must not look back, or worse yet, you must not carry that heavy baggage around with

you. So you didn't get the best marks in school, so you didn't get that job, so you didn't save enough money, so you didn't, so you didn't, so you didn't... so what?! Forget about it! Take the lessons from those experiences and learn from them, they are key to improving yourself.

Kick all those positive energy-drainers out to the curb. If you really want to live a positive life, you must put all your focus into it. What you do makes a difference. What you do is an important part of the fabric of life. Your actions or non-actions have an impact on not only yourself but those around you too. If you find yourself surrounded by those negative energy-drainers, the whiners in the crowd, just remove yourself from that situation. Walk away. Take action and take responsibility for your actions. Lead by example. Your behavior is what you have control of and without trying, your positive actions are sending out powerfully positive message to others.

If you feel weighed down, get rid of the anchor so that you can set sail. To begin, it is a good exercise to sit yourself down and do some soul searching. Make a list of what you believe are all the negative things that have happened to you and be honest with yourself. See the lessons in what went wrong, recognize what you learned and now get rid of the rest. You need to say goodbye to the rubbish before you can start to open your mind to the possibilities. After you have come to terms with everything on your list, your next step is to destroy it. Burn it, tear it up, cut it up into tiny pieces or put it into the shredder. By doing this, you will be closing the book on that chapter of your life experience; you will be cleansing your system of some very negative energy. Only then will you be able to move forward effectively and embrace life.

3. Know yourself. Focus on what makes you a good person. Analyze your strengths and your weaknesses. Celebrate

your strengths and be honest with yourself about your weaknesses to see where you can improve. Concentrate on your potential and believe that you are capable of greatness.

4. As you greet each day, be thankful for the fact that you are alive and ready to begin another day. Be thankful for even the simplest of things in life; the warmth of the sun, the beauty of a flower, the sound of birds singing, etc.

5. Have appreciation for your life experiences to date, for they have given you experience and shaped you and with each day, you have the chance to continue building on that.

6. Dream big, go for it, don't limit yourself, and find inspiration to help you continue to move forward towards your goal.

7. Create an action plan, because it is best to do a little each day. Set goals and write them down no matter how small. In university studies, it's proven that those that write out goals actually follow through with their plans by 200% over those that don't. As you check off your list of accomplishments, keep in mind that you are that much closer to where you are aiming.

8. Do a monthly audit check, this will help you keep on track and reinforce your goals. It will help you stay focused.

9. Create a wish list for the future you envision. Start off by jotting down, in point form, some of the things you'd like to do in your life, places to go, people to meet, vacations spots to visit, etc.

10. Reward yourself along the way, keep yourself motivated by recognizing and acknowledging your achievements, whether they are big or small.

SPARKLE
BE PASSIONATE

- CHAPTER TWO -

PASSION PRODUCES

"Be passionate about life, when you are, you will find your actions will open all sorts of possibilities for you to succeed."
Barbara Berezowski

As the saying goes, "Love makes the World Go'Round" and it's because love is a very powerful force. We all have it in us and we need to share it. Even without knowing it, you share love everyday in the little things you do. Just think, you have the opportunity to spread love and joy to others every day so you should be doing just that. Always! The only thing better than giving love, is receiving it. Use this as inspiration to make everyday better than the one before.

I know we are all busy, going about our daily tasks, sometimes in a mad rush, with no time to think. We miss meetings with friends because of work, we sometimes skip meals because of deadlines and there are times when we should take a vacation and cancel that too. Stress is a major concern in today's society and there are too many of us falling by the wayside as a result. Learn to handle matters in a more reasonable way. Don't lose perspective on life, and be kinder to yourself. How can you function effectively if you continue living at this pace? How can you be healthy living with all this stress and negativity? To experience an exceptional life on the outside, you must nurture exceptionally positive values on the inside. You cannot be angry or resentful and expect to achieve true happiness.

Even without knowing it, you share love every day in the little things you do.

It's a cliché but stop and smell the roses. Remember to take the time to relax and breathe. Love life, love your family, love your significant other, love your pets, love your friends and even your enemies. You must put yourself into a better place and be in a positive frame of mind, at all times. Know that we all have an incredible amount of infinite love inside of us and we were given that gift to share.

Love is happiness. Disperse some of that powerful energy throughout your daily routine with everyone you come across today and every day. Be passionate about life, when you are, you will find your actions will open all sorts of possibilities for you to succeed. You have another chance every day to start over. As you awaken, decide to be the best you can be. If you failed the day before, it doesn't matter because you tried. Today you will have the chance to try again. With this attitude, you will eventually succeed.

You need to believe in yourself. You will come to understand that your outside need for approval is what holds you back. Be willing to stop looking out there and look inward instead, your entire life will change. You will begin to stand taller and you will learn to find your source of peace and purpose from an inward condition. Your neediness will melt away, your insecurity will weaken and your self-doubt will transform into self-assurance. As an athlete, I can tell you that you must think this way. You must always be in that training mode. Visualize your destination, you will arrive.

It's About Love and Inspiration

A smile, a thank you, a compliment, a helping hand, giving an ear to listen, giving a shoulder to cry on, these are all the little things that you can do. Share your goodness and love with everyone you meet, even if it is someone you've just met. A warm, heartfelt, sincere greeting and a big beautiful smile have a tremendous effect. That is my simple inspirational message to you.

It doesn't take much effort to share love and the surprising thing is that the level of love in you to give will never run out. The love tank is NEVER empty. The more you share of yourself and the more love you give out, the more love comes back to you! Find inspiration in that fact. It's an unlimited supply; it's a never-ending cycle. Be happy and share the love!

Valentine's Day is a day to express love and affection. Loved ones everywhere, both young and old, rejoice in the fact that they have found that special someone to share their life with. Traditionally, it is a day for sweethearts and is celebrated with cards, letters, hearts, flowers, chocolate and jewellery. How nice, another chance to celebrate the beautiful things in life.

To my dismay, I hear so many complaints about

the day; "It's so commercial!" and "Oh it's just another excuse for the stores to hike up the prices of roses," etc. Personally, I am a fan of Valentine's Day, but not merely for the tokens and gifts expressing love. It is for the message of the occasion itself. It delivers such a positive message. I am writing about Valentine's Day as an example to stress that you not lose sight of the purpose and the importance of showing kindness and affection and if you're passionate about life, you'll understand that feeling and continue it through the whole year. All gifts from the heart, whether they are tangible or little acts of kindness, show others how much you care and appreciate them.

There are so many ways of expressing your love and you can be really creative in your delivery. This is a big world and life is full of ups and downs but through it all, there is one universal emotion that helps you get through it… LOVE.

Always remember that LOVE is the core to everything wonderful. Anything and everything is possible when you remember to add a bit of love into the recipe. Celebrate your love each and everyday. Do it by expressing your feelings and thinking of little things to do to show how you feel. Make a cup of coffee for your mate or leave a little love note before you go off to work. Be creative and have fun. Use your imagination when thinking up different ways to show how you feel… always. If you live your life with goodness and gratitude, you will realize that love is all around you.

Let your actions be that ray of sunshine in someone's day. When you have a passion for life and you are feeling good, it is so easy to be generous with that emotion. Love, in all its forms is meant to be shared.

Be Young at Heart and Live an Inspirational Life

Each of us has been given the wonderful gift of living and breathing and being and it should never be taken for granted. Life is a series of opportunities. It is up to us to learn and grow and flourish from life's experiences and we have the chance to make it inspirational. It makes good sense to not waste the opportunities that are presented to us each and every day. Remember the simple happiness in your heart as a child and realize it's still there. The young at heart know it and so should you. Tap into it and allow the energy to flow.

Danny Kaye, one of Hollywood's funniest actor/comedians, was young at heart and that was evident in his movies. He had a great quote; "Life is a big blank canvas; throw all the paint on it you can."

It is a wonderfully positive description of how he saw life as a precious gift, and it is up to you to create your own masterpiece with what you do and how you live.

Living your life in a positive and productive way is a great way to contribute to society. Be a contributor to life and be inspirational to others. Your input matters a great deal and helps produce our very fabric of existence. Be proud of yourself and of your contributions. Stay young at heart and enjoy everything life has to offer. You will be inspiring others around you to do the same.

Helpful tips for staying young at heart and living a good life

Live... always staying young; we all have an inner child within us, don't ever stifle that pure happiness and outlook on life you had as a child.

Love... yourself, love others; always love with everything that you have and be willing to forgive.

Laugh... as often as you can, for as long as you can and as loud as you can; laughter is the best medicine.

Be positive... for tomorrow is another day.

Appreciate... surrounding yourself with the things that you love; take in the beauty of your favorite things.

Play... doing the things you enjoy doing; make time to enjoy your hobbies.

Enjoy... the simple things; life doesn't have to be so complicated.

Grow... by never stopping to learn, keep your mind active; the brain is a muscle we must exercise.

Be happy... staying cheerful and keep close to your cheerful friends; keep the positive energy going, negativity can drain your batteries.

Cherish... your health; good health is something to be thankful for, you can't put a price tag on health.

Value... your family and home life—mothers, fathers, sons, daughters, brothers, sisters, cousins, etc.

Be kind... to others; be good to people and animals and the environment.

Passion produces positivity, and with that, anything is possible.

BE POSITIVE

- CHAPTER THREE -

A POSITIVE ATTITUDE IS AN ESSENTIAL LIFE STRATEGY

"To get up each morning with the resolve to be happy is to set our own conditions to the events of each day. To do this is to condition circumstances instead of being conditioned by them."

Ralph Waldo Emerson

You are capable of great achievement. You must always be in a positive state to nurture your dreams. Think of that seedling you planted last spring. How many times did you feed it and water it hoping to see it grow? Along with the anticipation of wanting to see the first little sprout peeking up through the soil, you were sending positive thoughts in the process, without even knowing it. I am sure you never once thought, while you were caring for it, that the seedling was not going to grow. You need to have a positive outlook and apply that attitude to whatever you attempt.

Your positive action will always result in a positive reaction. Can you imagine what the outcome might be if I entered a competition with a negative attitude and without believing in myself? "Why am I here?" "I don't think I'm good enough" "Oh, I know I'm going to fail!" The effect of this kind of thinking is like jumping into the deepest part of a lake with an anchor tied around my feet and expect to swim to shore with ease. It's not likely going to happen.

When you watch a sporting event on TV, what you are watching are athletes putting their heart and soul into their dream. They tirelessly train to better themselves and their preparation includes not only development of their physical bodies but their mental state as well. There is no room for self-doubt because their focus is on everything positive. You must believe in what you think, feel, say and do. Remember your base core, your energy source, deep within you, is positive. Build on that. Don't go through life covering it up and extinguishing the flame with negativity and doubt.

Your positive action will always result in a positive reaction.

There is goodness with a positive energy living within you. Connect with it, acknowledge it, express it and share it with everyone around you. By doing so, you will notice that your actions create corresponding goodness. You will succeed and everyone around you will cheer. When you recognize and engage the goodness and positive energy within you, you are empowered to do great things.

Life is precious because time is short. Whether you are fortunate enough to live to be 100 or not, live each and every day to its fullest. Where there is a hurdle in life, think your way through it to find a solution and use your energy to accentuate the positive. Learn from each experience.

When I need motivation, I seek out inspiration. I always find something wonderful in the daily affirmations by Wayne Dyer, Ph.D. He is an internationally renowned author and speaker in the field of self-development.

"With everything that has happened to you, you can either feel sorry for yourself or treat what has happened as a gift. Everything is either an opportunity to grow or an obstacle to keep you from growing. You get to choose."

Dr. Wayne Dyer

Always look at the big picture and find what is good about it and how you can make it even better. It is so important to look at life in a positive way because it feeds our happiness and our energy.

You heard the alarm clock this morning and woke up, right? That is a gift, an opportunity to experience a brand new day. Isn't that wonderful? Yes, it is! I am here to write this and you are here to read this. We are living and breathing and sharing and that is a very good thing. Start feeling gratitude for that positive fact today. There are so many different ways to maintain a positive attitude and it is essential for a better life.

When you say "How are you?" to someone, mean it. Wait for, and really be interested in, the answer. It amazes me how so many people say that little phrase everyday, sometimes in passing, and they never hear or even wait for the answer. Too busy or they just don't think to listen. On the flip side, when someone asks you how you are, be grateful for that act in itself and be gracious. Answering by listing all of things wrong with you is not keeping with the life plan of being positive.

Maxine Taylor, Georgia's first Licensed Astrologer, has written a wonderful book, *Move Into The Magic*. In it, she shares the transformational methods she teaches. She empowers you to rediscover your passion. It is a powerful book and she has graciously given me permission to share an excerpt with you:

> *"You are infinite, immortal, majestic, powerful, awesome, gloriously beautiful, radiantly healthy, abundantly wealthy Spirit in physical form. You are God in an earthbound body. This is the truth. Anything else is a lie. You have come here with a thrilling mission. When you discover and express your mission, you move into the Magic—the Magic that is you."*
>
> Maxine Taylor,
> Astrologer, Spiritual Healer and Author

Maxine's message is an extremely positive one and it will also empower you to learn and grow and develop. You should try to expand your knowledge at every chance. It's another opportunity for you to grow. Delivering a positive message is such a good practice with so many benefits, for both the giver and the receiver. Think of it as the water and nutrients you give your garden, to help it blossom. I am a strong believer in karma. What goes around comes around. There is a very magnetic quality about the force of positivity. When you have positive thoughts and look at life in this way, an amazing thing happens. Positive things start coming back at you.

Positive Sparkle Tips

Have faith in the power of YOU.

Always think positive. (The glass half full vs. half empty.) Stop thinking and saying "Why Me?" and turn it into "Why not?'

Be good. Always give it your best effort.

Be kind. Lend a helping hand.

Treat everyone around you in a manner that is respectful and accepting.

Live your life by giving out what you want to receive.

Look for little ways to make this world a happier place.

Smile. You will look better, feel better and you'll receive smiles in return.

Take Decisive Action

This leads to feeling exuberant and full of life. Your general level of enthusiasm may also increase. A good way to apply these feelings is to focus your attention on opportunities for growth and advancement. Take decisive action towards any of your goals and you will have beneficial outcomes. You may wish to think about ways you could be bolder in your actions, why not apply for a new job or expand your personal goals. Allow yourself to feel excited about what you are doing. This will make your efforts all the more enjoyable and satisfying when you do succeed.

Pursuing your dreams with exuberance, optimism, and enthusiasm adds powerful energy to your efforts. While taking any action toward the achievement of your goals is likely to be beneficial, infusing your actions with a high level of energy can jump-start your efforts into high gear. Your enthusiasm could give you the inspiration and motivation you need to do what it takes to manifest what you want. By focusing your enthusiastic mind-set on furthering your goals, you will be able to take powerful steps toward the fulfillment of your dreams. Live each day to the best of your ability and then go beyond that. Go the extra mile and see what you can do to make this world a better place. You can make a difference. Think of it as inspirational acceptance and be at peace.

Be satisfied with what you can control and what you can do. When you come up against a problem or challenge… don't waste your precious time worrying about something that is beyond your control. Follow your own path. Look at every situation as an opportunity to further your development. Never think you can't. Don't limit yourself with negative thoughts. Be creative and be inspired to find ways to come to some resolve. No matter the outcome, you will be successful because you handled it.

Let the negative thoughts go. Like a waterfall, it is essential to let all negativity be swept away like the water going over the edge… just let it go. You don't want any negativity to enter your positive state of mind. Be an inspiration to others. Your life, and the lives of those around you, will be so enriched by the power of the positive.

Positive Sparkle Tips

1. **Be Kind**

Showing kindness is a great gift to share with people. Family, friends, co-workers and even strangers are all included in this great big circle of acquaintances we interact with. A smile, a greeting, a compliment, a hug, these are all the little things you can do on a daily basis. It doesn't take much effort and it will have a very positive effect on everyone, you included. When driving, don't be in such a rush or be so self-absorbed that you forget to say thank you to another driver for showing you a courtesy. It makes me crazy to see a motorist not even lift their hand to signal a quick "Thanks"... not because it is law and someone has broken it but because it makes me realize how unaware some people have become. It can be reversed, one person at a time. For every act of kindness, there will be another that is made more aware.

2. **Be Happy**

As you awake each day, make the choice to be happy. Happiness is contagious. You have the ability to bring happiness to others just by being happy. You will find that by changing your attitude to a positive one, you will be going through life as a happy person. It's a natural phenomenon.

3. **Be Joyful**

Don't be afraid to live, love and laugh! It's true: "laughter is the best medicine." You can feel joy in so many ways and in so many places. Enthusiasm and excitement are feelings of being joyful; don't be afraid to show it. It's as simple as enjoying the sound of a baby's laughter, or the anticipated dinner out with your friends. Why, you can even experience joy by singing along to your favorite song on your car radio, turn up the volume and just let go.

4. **Be Grateful**
It is so important to show appreciation and gratitude. There are countless reasons to be grateful. Your health, your job, your children, your friends, or for the coffee someone just bought you unexpectedly, and so on. Even if you're facing a challenge of some kind at the moment, be grateful that you are here on earth to be facing it. By actively living positively, you will find a solution.

5. **Be Generous**
Money is usually the first thing many think of when they think about generosity. It's great to help someone out financially if they need it and you can afford to without creating a hardship for yourself, however generosity isn't just associated with money. You can be extremely generous with your time, your experiences, your knowledge, your attention to others. There are so many ways to lend a helping hand when someone needs it and even when they say they don't.

KINDNESS MATTERS

Be kind and joyful; be generous and feel gratitude, and you will have a mindset that is positive.

By living your life this way, you will be more at peace. You will be in a better place to handle the chaos around you. Yes, things will continue to happen that will greatly challenge you but you will be in a much better place spiritually, to better handle what comes your way. A positive attitude will strengthen you and prepare you to turn challenges into opportunities.

SPARKLE
BE ALIVE

- CHAPTER FOUR -

REMEMBER TO LIVE IN THE MOMENT

"Begin doing what you want to do now. We are not living in eternity. We have only this moment, sparkling like a star in our hand—melting like a snowflake."

Francis Bacon, Sr. (Philosopher, 1561-1626)

There are many who, when asked, need to really concentrate and think back to a situation where they were consciously experiencing "a moment." If they have to really think that hard to remember it, chances are they were not living in the moment.

Life is too short. There's so much to do, to see and to experience. Without being aware of what is actually happening to you, life is whizzing by us at lightening speed. How many times have you heard, "where did the time go? How did they grow up so fast?"

Without actually taking in and absorbing those special moments in your life and realizing the magnitude of their importance, getting something from them is something that will not happen for you. Be motivated to make things better. Everyone has their task lists, their "honey-do" lists, the day-timers that are filled with appointments to keep, meetings to attend, deadlines to meet. This has become the norm. If this sounds like you, then what you must do is prioritize... not what task must be completed first but putting your life and relationships into proper order and perspective.

The biggest benefit of living in the moment is that your quality of life rises through the roof. The first step of living in the moment is awareness. Know who you are, your strengths and your weaknesses. Analyze your inner spirit and focus on being a good human being. Be kind and enjoy the people around you. Realize that you have love in you and it is there to share in many different kinds of ways. Do something nice for someone today... just because.

The biggest benefit of living in the moment is that your quality of life rises through the roof.

Don't be so caught up in the chores of life that you forget to live it. Don't ignore the opportunities that are the special moments in time, they present themselves to you as something to cherish. As an example, when your child asks you to play catch, don't hesitate to say "sure, let's do it." Know that you can finish that report later.

You may not realize it but you already have taken the time to capture some special moments in life. Have you ever grabbed your camera and taken a picture? Isn't that the same? You are realizing that something is special and wonderful and you want to remember it. Living in the moment is doing just that with your brain and your heart. Firstly, there is the realization of it, then the conscious effort to appreciate it and then to lock it away in the memory bank.

Live your life in the moment, appreciate what is happening around you and believe that you are exactly where you are in that moment because you were meant to be there. Everything else will fall into place. Getting the tasks done, paying your bills on time, being somewhere to catch a plane or bus or train, those are things that will fall into place eventually. It is more important to use your energy to serve you first.

Be aware of what goes on around you. There are always special moments to be had, all around you.

Keep a journal. Jot down those special moments in life that made a big impact on you.

Celebrate your moments. Realize that life has great things to offer, be open to accept it.

Spread the joy. Share your experiences and your stories.

Live with appreciation and gratitude. There will be no regrets that you missed out on something along the way.

Be good to yourself, practice relaxation to handle stress.

As an athlete, I was trained by the best skating coaches, choreographers, fitness instructors and physiotherapists. They all agreed that the best way to take care of the body and mind and soul was through proper stretching, warm up, exertion, resting, physical training, proper nutrition, good time management skills and relaxation.

You are the soul and your body is the vessel. You have the responsibility to do the best you can as far as keeping that vessel running smoothly. There is good stress and there is bad stress and you need to handle everything to ensure there is a balance. If not, stress can be very damaging. Stress has a negative impact on your body, just like salt can eat through metal and cause rust on your car. Whether you are an athlete, a butcher, a baker, or a candlestick maker, it is important for you to remember to incorporate relaxation into your daily life to better handle stress. I would like to share one amazing relaxation technique I learned as an athlete. It's called Body Scan Meditation. I still practice it today, especially when I find my stress levels are a bit too much to handle.

Give it a try. I've included an outline for you to follow.

Body Scan Meditation for Stress Relief

This is a simple relaxation technique that you can do at home or away on vacation.

Here's how to do it:

- Get your yoga mat, if you have one, and find a spot on the floor in a quiet room.
- Play some soft spa-like music to help the mood.
- Lie on your back, legs uncrossed, arms relaxed at your sides, eyes closed.
- Focus on your breathing, allowing your stomach to rise as you inhale and fall as you exhale. Breathe deeply for about two minutes, until you start to feel comfortable and relaxed.
- Turn your focus to the toes of your right foot. Notice any sensations you feel while continuing to also focus on your breathing. Imagine each deep breath flowing to your toes. Remain focused on this area for one to two minutes.
- Move your focus to the sole of your right foot. Tune in to any sensations you feel in that part of your body and imagine

each breath flowing from the sole of your foot.

- After one or two minutes, move your focus to your right ankle and repeat.
- Move to your calf, knee, thigh, hip, and then repeat the sequence for your left leg.
- From there, move up the torso, through the lower back and abdomen, the upper back and chest, and the shoulders. Pay close attention to any area of the body that causes you pain or discomfort.
- Move your focus to the fingers on your right hand and then move up to the wrist, forearm, elbow, upper arm, and shoulder.
- Repeat for your left arm.
- Then move through the neck and throat, and finally all the regions of your face, the back of the head, and the top of the head. Pay close attention to your jaw, chin, lips, tongue, nose, cheeks, eyes, forehead, temples and scalp. When you reach the very top of your head, let your breath reach out beyond your body and imagine yourself completely relaxed.
- After completing the body scan, rest for a while in silence and stillness, noting how your body feels. Then open your eyes slowly.
- Have a "feel good" stretch and you are done and the stress and tension are now out the door!

Life is wonderful, so live in the moment and take it all in. When you are motivated to appreciate the beauty of life, you become in touch with it and you will be amazed at how much is really going on around you that you've never noticed before. Let your brain and heart capture those special moments. You will feel happiness, be fulfilled and find peace. You will love life by experiencing those special moments and you will have no regrets.

Lighten Up! Stop Taking Yourself So Seriously

Learn to laugh at yourself and enjoy life all the more. We are all human, we all make mistakes. Don't be so serious that you can't forgive yourself. Give yourself permission to laugh. In fact, life becomes more fun when you learn to laugh at yourself. My friends have even pleaded with me to write a book on just the "oops" moments I have had because there have been many!! There have been things that I have said and done that simply make everyone around me burst out laughing. There is nothing wrong with that as long as you are all laughing together. Most of the time it is me that starts the laugh first. When you have one of "those moments," don't hold back, just laugh it off. Don't be so serious that you can't forgive yourself for the silly mistakes you may make along the way.

Like it or not, life can be very short. You should consciously make the decision to enjoy the ride and make the best of everyday. We are all born with an inner energy. This energy source starts off with a positive charge. We are born with that charge. It is the actions of a person or how a person chooses to deal with various situations in their life that determines if this energy source remains in a positive state or if they allow negativity into the equation.

There will always be good and bad in life and it is what we decide to do and make of it that determines who we are. I'm sure you've heard that the Chinese have known about this for centuries. It's called the Ying and Yang of Life. Everything must have a perfect balance to be effective. Recognize the fact that you are in control of how you will be affected by the events around you. Choose to take things in stride and deal with the issues that come your way in an effective manner. The goal is to properly deal with day-to-day issues by finding a perfect balance, so that you don't tip the scale because that's when problems start. It is optimism that gives us a fighting chance.

Stress is not a healthy thing to deal with. It has far-reaching damaging affects on the body. To keep your stress at a manageable level, use any technique you prefer but remember to relax. A long soak in a hot bath is another a good practice. Light some candles, play some soft music and enjoy your down time. Lighten up, have fun and don't be so serious that you forget to laugh. They say a smile is better than medicine and it is so true. Think of it this way… do things get better or go away faster if you fret? I think not! Why bother fretting over something that has happened that you can't change or beating yourself up over something that is beyond your control? That's just negative, useless energy and it will slowly devour you. Don't allow that to happen. Always remember that life is a sweet and wonderful gift and be inspired by that. You make of it what you can, just keep on keepin' on.

So the next time you happen to take the wrong turn or flub your lines or strike out, get over it quickly. Do not beat yourself up over it. It happens. You are far better off if you choose to deal with things right away. As a case in point; in skating, falling down is part of the sport. Even though the goal is to finish your performance flawlessly, a fall can occur. It's the nature of the beast but skaters are taught to get up immediately and to stay in the zone and focus on the job at hand… Finishing the program to the best of your ability. If "the fall" is what you continue to focus on, then how can you continue successfully with what's still to come? Put a big red bow on those negative feelings and kick them to the curb! Move on and continue on your path to greatness! Take each moment in life and give it your full attention.

BE INSPIRED

- CHAPTER FIVE -

KNOW THAT YOU CAN FOLLOW YOUR DREAM

"Everyone's a star and deserves the right to twinkle."
Marilyn Monroe

Inspiration is the icing on a cake. All it takes is an idea, a thought, a wish, a dream; that added element to make it a reality and to see that creation of yours develop into something real and wonderful. How many times has a thought crossed your mind and a feeling of excitement along with it?

If you take your dream, your thought, that moment in time, then add inspiration and focus to it, can you imagine what may lie ahead? The opportunities are out there and the possibilities are endless. Think big, be creative. Don't ever think your idea is not good enough! With proper guidelines and development, the sky is the limit.

In my case, I found my inspiration many moons ago. It happened when I went to see the Ice Follies, as a seven year old. Shipstads and Johnson's Ice Follies was an Ice Show that travelled across North America. It was a glamorous Hollywood style extravaganza on ice and the company of talented ice skaters would come to town for two weeks every year and appear at Toronto's Maple Leaf Gardens. I was mesmerized by the lights and sounds and excitement of the gorgeous skaters in their beautiful costumes with all the brilliant colors and sparkling sequins.

I was hooked as soon as the band started up and the spotlights hit their twirling targets out on that ice surface. That was it for me. I remember thinking "I want to do this when I grow up." I never lost that feeling. Deep within me, I knew it was set as my goal from that very moment. There was no doubt in my mind; that was what I wanted more than anything and I was going to do what I had to do to get there.

I am convinced that there is a tremendous power in your thoughts and in your dreams. Why? I am convinced because I achieved it. I became a Star in that very same show. I travelled across North America, along with so many great skaters, in Shipstads and Johnson's Ice Follies. Just as I had envisioned it as a young girl, I came to town and appeared in the Hollywood style extravaganza on ice at Toronto's Maple Leaf Gardens. I was so grateful that I secretly decided to do something special. With every performance, I made it a point to pick out a little girl in the front row, no matter what city we were playing at the time, and smiled at her specifically. I was hoping to ignite a similar dream for her.

What gets in the way of those moments of creativity from blossoming into something wonderful, are the feelings of self-doubt and negativity. Everyone on this earth is a unique individual, endowed with many various abilities and has the capability of doing great things. Focus, drive and determination mixed in with knowledge, inspiration and potential will make any person unstoppable in their individual quest.

You can do it, look at life in a positive way and never doubt yourself for a minute. Everything is possible and you can be a success. We all have that potential. Don't get me wrong, it is normal to feel apprehensive at times, but shake it off and re-focus on what your desire is and go for it. Remind yourself of the reason why you set out on this mission of yours and take positive action everyday. Have patience and do a little at a time. Just like how a baby learns how to crawl before he or she can walk, it's a natural progression. From birth on, we take everything step by step and before we even realize it, we are running, skipping, jumping and skating. It's the same principle with any venture, do a little at a time and you will get there. Your goals and dreams, that are deep within you, are definite possibilities and they are there to be acted upon and nurtured. Never lose sight of that.

It is crucial to stay positive and search out only those that will offer encouragement and positive, constructive advice.

You can find inspiration anywhere. You may come across it by surprise when you're not even searching for it or sometimes you may be on a mission for it. Inspiration will happen and when it does, when you hear the words that ignite that flame for you, take action. Use that to propel yourself to where you want to be. That is all you need to empower yourself to go after your dream. It is crucial to stay positive and search out only those that will offer encouragement and positive, constructive advice. Don't bother giving any of the negative nay-sayers out there the chance to burst your bubble.

Choose to stay on your own path to achieve what it is you are after. Seek out motivational materials and inspirational speakers and be open to suggestions. Never give up on your dream even though the road may get bumpy from time to time along the way. Expect those bumps and don't let that frustrate you. Don't be resistant to change; step out of your comfort zone and see how far you can go. Take the challenges that you face and change them into opportunities to get better. You have the capability to do great things, practice and perseverance sprinkled with motivation is the formula to stick to.

Develop a Life Strategy

How do you do that?

Create a wish list for yourself. Think of it as your *Personal Development Plan.*

Begin by writing down what you would like to do if you had a chance to do it and nothing was holding you back. Take a trip; find a job; learn a new skill; speak another language; start a hobby, etc. Just write, let your mind wander to a place you want to be. To help you get started, you can use this exercise below. Use this as a guideline or action list and write down what comes to mind as you answer the following questions. Give yourself a few days to think, if need be.

By the time you get to the end of this exercise, come up with a realistic Start Date to begin your Personal Development. Apply your ideas and develop that strategy and you'll be on your way on your personal roadmap to success. You can add or delete whatever you like and I suggest you keep it so that you can re-visit it from time to time to keep yourself on the right path.

What About You?

What makes you great? What are your strengths? What are you passionate about? How can you develop? How can you improve? What one small thing would you do to change or improve your character or personality? Would you like to be a bit more outgoing? More patient? Accepting? When you have it in mind, what steps can you take to get there?

What About Your Health?

How is your health? What is one small thing you could do to improve your health? Can you cut down on your portion sizes? Is there a particular food you should stay away from? An extra day of exercise you could throw in the routine? When was the last time you saw your doctor for a check up? Write down your next healthy living goal and the action you'll take to make it happen.

What About Your Career?

Are you happy with your job? What one small thing could you do to change or improve your career? Is there another position you would like to apply for? Whatever it is, write it down and don't leave anything out.

What about Your _________ ?

(I left this one blank for you. You may have something specific in mind that you would like to plan out.) What one small thing could you do to change or improve your ____________? Is there something you always wanted to try? Have you always wanted to run your own business? What's your passion? Do you need to find a teacher? Whatever it is, write it down and match it with a specific action you can take within a few days to make it happen.

____

____

____

____

____

One last thing to do…

Create a Positivity Board to help you visualize your goal.

What is your passion? What pulls on your heart strings? What's your life's mission? Is there something you've always wanted to do or someplace you've just got to get to? Have you dreamt of this for yourself? Start your journey towards making this a reality by writing down your ideas. Take these ideas and create a Positivity Board to keep that dream alive.

Hang a corkboard, and get some colorful thumb tacks. Now pin up newspaper articles, photographs, fortune cookie quotes, whatever is in line with your passion. You want to see it! Use this as a constant reminder to learn and grow and develop into what you want to be and then go out and follow your dream.

It's all about visualization. It's a powerful tool. Close your eyes and visualize in your mind, everything that you want to be or everything that you want to do. Once you have your Positivity

Board in place, you'll have something tangible to work with, to help you visualize your goal.

Be excited at the prospect of following your dream. Be dedicated to the follow-through process. Look to others that can help guide you. Know that you can accomplish great things, if you put forth the effort. Believe in yourself, find inspiration and enjoy the experience of following your dream.

Your Plan, Your Vision

Stay positive and focused on your plan, keep working on it, consistency is key. Don't give up, even if it means that a revision to your plan may be necessary. You will achieve what you set out to do. Your positive attitude and dedicated work effort will pay off. The tasks will be completed and you will be accomplishing. You can experience an outstanding life if you constantly and persistently envision an outstanding life. Believe in yourself and believe in your vision. When you look at life with a positive focus, your actions will have a positive outcome.

It is never too late to begin a new plan. Find inspiration, think about what you'd like to do, or fix, or improve, or change. Let this year be the year you finally quit smoking, start and stick to a workout plan, live a healthier lifestyle, manage your finances in a better way or start a new career. Whatever your plan is, believe in yourself, get 'er started, stay committed and get 'er done.

Be honest and accountable to yourself, by doing so, you will set goals with a higher chance of success. Be inspired by the very thought that you are taking a proactive approach to better your life. Firstly, you need to let go of everything negative when setting your sights on success. To do that, you will want to reflect on the year gone by and give yourself a report card. What did you do well? Where could you have improved? Did you meet and/or succeed your expectations? Look at the pros and cons and develop a plan that will work best to give you the chance to succeed.

Look back to the things that could have gone better for you and analyze the data. Sometimes, the failures can be the most powerful learning tools we have. Figure out why something went wrong and see where the opportunities lie to turn things around. On the other hand, review your successes and see how to apply that strategy to your other ventures. There is no need to over complicate things, plain and simple is the best way, always. When trying to organize your thoughts, your plans, your goals, use the K.I.S.S. method ("Keep It Simple, Stupid"). "Less is more," as they say.

Be Adventurous

If you keep doing what you've always done, then how can you expect anything to be better or different? Try to do a little more than you've done in the past and you will soon find yourself doing more. You will feel more powerful after you challenge yourself and succeed.

From the most difficult situations, you can build your biggest successes. When you take on any obstacle and successfully find your way through, you will be so energized. Your comfort zone will increase in size and you will feel brave enough to keep moving forward. Remember, it's one step at a time and you will eventually get to where you want to go. With every step, you are overcoming a fear and that is already an accomplishment. Now take that and build on it. Just keep going!

Find a mentor, a teacher or a coach to help you achieve

your goal. They can help by guiding you to the finish line. They won't do the work for you but they will motivate you and inspire you to find the way. No reason to be shy, they would be happy to assist you. As you gain more confidence, you can try things on your own and you will become more comfortable.

Life can be complicated but with patience and persistence and with the realization that a positive attitude is the most powerful tool in your toolbox, you will take on the challenges you come up against and you will find solutions.

When setting a goal, it is important to give it a chance to work. If your goal is to change a bad habit, you're making a good decision. It's a better life choice. Do not think of it as giving something up because you're adding negativity to the process. When making that resolution, think of the exercise as something that will benefit you greatly. You will feel deprived if your focus will be on the "giving up something." Instead of thinking that way, concentrate on the exciting feeling of taking a chance in life to make things better. Your life, your business, your situation will improve and the greatness that will be realized will be well worth the courage and effort. Be positive and allow that good energy to propel you forward. Go out and get what you want. Go for it and wow the crowd!

Take responsibility for your actions. Be inspired by your faith and your beliefs. Work to develop and build on your strengths as a good person. No matter how you choose to find inspiration and motivation, it's good to find strength and purpose in it.

Great Sources of Inspiration

Given the fact, that in today's world, so many of us are bogged down with busy schedules, impossible deadlines, never-ending lists of things to do and not enough hours in the day to get everything done, we must find a better way. Stress is the killer of everything good so it is imperative to slow down, take a step back and find a better way to handle things. There are great sources of inspiration available in this world to help you cope.

Just imagine, the alarm goes off but you didn't hear it. Slept in again! Mad dash to the shower, gulp down a few sips of coffee… no time for breakfast, "I'll get something later," you think. Get out to the car and find Mother Nature's beautiful gift of an inch of snow and ice blanketing your world. (Had to put that one in there, I'm from Canada, eh?!)

You start the car, heater and defroster at full blast but still not doing it's job fast enough for you, so you decide to scrap a little patch of the windshield, just big enough to see through, as if you were in some enclosed bunker. Then you notice the gas gauge is on the big "E". Off to the gas station you go, setting yourself back another 15 minutes! Can you feel the stress level rising? All this and you haven't even attempted that morning rush hour traffic. Sound familiar?

Unfortunately, it does. This is a common scenario for too many. What you must all do, is slow down and find a better way to cope with today's pressures. After all, you can have better control if you put things into proper perspective.

Look for inspiration. Take in the beauty of life. There is inspiration to be found in the beauty of everyday things. Look around you. When you are in a mad dash to get to there from here and here to there and back again, you are missing opportunities to take in the inspiring moments.
After a good night's sleep, get up a little earlier to sit and relax and savor that flavor of your coffee, breathe in that wonderful aroma as you greet another day. Enjoy a good breakfast. Leave a little earlier so you won't feel rushed. Make a commitment

to take better care of yourself; it will not only benefit you but all those around you as well.

Leaving the house, better prepared to handle the events of the day ahead, you will now notice things around you. These things will serve as inspiration to you, if you would just be open-minded enough to notice.

Even while you are sitting in a traffic jam or stopped at a red light, you can now look around you and find inspiration in the beauty of life. There are sights, sounds, smells… use your senses and become aware of them. Listen to those birds singing; visually take in the vibrant colors of the flowers in summer or the beauty of a crisp white, sparkling blanket of snow in winter. Feel the warmth of the sun on your face and be grateful for all these things.

You will find inspiration in this exercise itself, as it will strengthen your spirit and improve your overall attitude. It's these little things in life you should not ignore because after all, they are what make life so wonderful. Slow down, be appreciative for what you have and make life's journey a happy one. Smile. You will have a better day, a better life, and better health.

SPARKLE
BE OUTSTANDING

- CHAPTER SIX -

LET POSITIVE PEOPLE SHOW YOU THE WAY

"When your positive values become your behavior, that's when you'll feel their true power."
Ralph Marston

When you are feeling overwhelmed by work, problems, details, bills, worries, help yourself through the stressful situations and by making the journey a little more enjoyable. Believe it or not, there is a simple solution to making that happen. Each and everyday of your life, you are given opportunities to make things happen, to deal with things in a better way and to make the most of any situation. Turn your life into a happy journey and enjoy each moment. Besides relaxation techniques (like the Body Meditation exercise I mentioned in Chapter 4), there are a few simple things you can do to be ready to handle the everyday stresses of life.

Stay positive. Develop and maintain an outlook that is positive. Find motivation to get into that way of thinking. Look to motivational messages, quotes, stories to lift your spirits up. There are millions of these in books and magazines and on the Internet these days.

Stay close to positive people and spend your time with them. Their positivity will rub off on you and you will find that it feels so good being positive that you'll want to remain there. The right choice is to go with the path that is good. Spend your time with the people that are well-adjusted and are happy. They have managed life's challenges and are still smiling. There's a positive message in their happy demeanor and be receptive to that.

Do not allow negativity to rent out any space in your life. Negative sensations can enter into your life and become the unwanted guest that won't leave, in even the most simplest of ways, if you let it. One such example is through the daily newscast. Ever notice that news programmers constantly focus on extremely negative stories and sensationalize even the smallest of events? Absorbing all that negativity, day in and day out, will only drag you down. Don't allow that to happen. You need to find a way to control how much of this you watch. I'm not saying you should never watch the news and live your life like an ostrich, with your head in a hole in the ground, just limit the quantity of the bad stuff you are exposed to daily and use good judgment to put things into proper perspective.

Surround yourself with everything positive. Do things that make you happy. Remember to have fun. Laughter is indeed the best medicine. Stress is accompanied with fear and panic. It is a well known fact that humor disengages fear because it changes your perspective both for past and present situations. I recently read that a research team from Loma Linda, California, conducted a study to see if laughter could boost the immune system and reduce the levels of three stress hormones, cortisol (the stress hormone), epinephrine (adrenaline), and dopac (a brain chemical which helps produce epinephrine). What they found in their research was that their subject group's blood levels showed that their detrimental stress hormones were reduced when they were in a state of anticipating a positive event. So keeping things positive is a good health benefit because it prepares you for the stresses of life.

Deal with your issues in an organized and planned out strategy. Take control of your debt and pay your bills on time. Be satisfied that you've tried your best and everything will fall nicely into place. Always add fun to the equation when taking on any task.

As I said, don't take everything so seriously. Season your life with humor because it has healing powers. Find a way to be able to laugh in life. Laughter is great medicine, a giggle or two now and then, allows you to be fully accepting of yourself, the good and the bad. Follow the lead of the positive souls out there. Positive people will guide you and you will find that having a great sense of humor is a wonderful way to handle life's stressful moments.

Smiling at the World

Have you ever tried to brighten someone's day with just a smile? It can and does happen. You have the ability to make others feel good, so why not give it a try? Whether you realize it or not… it's a feel good exercise for your soul and your face. Smile and the world smiles with you!

A smile is so powerful, you can even hear it! Really! When someone answers the phone with a smile… your senses pick up on that and it immediately sets a tone for a productive and positive conversation.

Life is too precious to be spending your days with a scowl on your face, so be pleasant, be happy and smile. We only have a set number of days to work with, while on this earth, so why not make the best of them?! Let's make our stay as pleasant as we can and why not spread that feeling around?

What makes one smile? It could be a joke, a thought, a memory but it all brings out inner joy! We all have it… for some, that inner joy is right there spilling over, for others, it is hidden away and loaded down with tons and tons of "other" stuff, but it's still there.

For all you hoarders of negativity out there… time to get rid of all that junk! Focus on thoughts that make you happy…those thoughts can be from an event as recent as today or it could be from memories locked inside you from when you were a child. You've grown up but it doesn't say anywhere, in the manual, that you can't be as free with your smile now as you once were when you were a kid.

Think pleasant thoughts to put yourself in a good mood. What do you enjoy? For me, it is summer. My mind just has to go to a beach somewhere and I am instantly inspired. I imagine how hot that sun feels and how refreshing that water must be. What does it do for me? It makes me smile on the inside and it makes me feel good. Try it; it inevitably results in others around you picking up on your positive energy.

It's extremely contagious, when someone smiles at you; it instantly makes you smile back. Go out and try it. Go out and smile at the world today. Give a smile to someone. It won't hurt you a bit and you will be doing both yourself and someone else a lot of good.

I have such confidence in the unbelievable potential that you possess and in the power of a Positive Attitude that I have set up a page for you to use as your personal Commitment Declaration. This is a tangible, formal commitment to serve as a reminder of this life transition. Are you ready to start living a positive life? Make a commitment to yourself to start anew. Making a pact with yourself to look at life with a renewed positive energy enforces self-trust and belief in your self worth. You can do this.

Positive Attitude Commitment

I, ______________________________, make the commitment to myself and to the world, to begin again and look at life with great appreciation and a renewed energy.

As of this date, _______________, I take responsibility for my own attitude and actions. I will be more aware of my boundless personal potential and choose to always view life with a Positive Attitude and show gratitude. I will *Win At Life and Positively Sparkle!*

Signed:______________________________________

Congratulations! Happy New Positive Life! Hand out the sunglasses... because you will sparkle!

"The purpose of life, after all, is to love it, to taste experience to the utmost, to reach out eagerly and without fear for newer and richer experience." ~Eleanor Roosevelt

BE GREAT

- CHAPTER SEVEN -

EVERY SUCCESS IS GREAT... IT DOESN'T NEED TO BE BIG!

"As someone aspiring to be an Olympian, your journey will take you through a roller coaster of joy, challenge, disappointment, physical injury, triumph, devastation and hopefully, victory. Kind of like life, isn't it? Except this journey is done with the whole world watching."

Scott Hamilton, 1984 Olympic Gold Medalist, Figure Skating

Is there something you really want to do but don't know how or where to begin? No matter what, there is always a way to get it done. Put aside all those lame excuses, objections and any other obstacles and just begin. Make it happen. Never give up; many achievements were accomplished by tired and discouraged people who kept on working. Not only that, they accepted their failed attempts and considered them as lessons. As a result, these people only got better because of them.

If you don't know how to go about making your dream a reality, then try to find someone who can teach you. If that is not possible, then figure out your own approach. Perhaps you had a dream that you discarded long ago because you didn't believe in the possibility of it. Think back to when you were first inspired by it. Try to recall what you felt at that moment.

Now, imagine an end result that you would like to have. Focus on that for a minute to charge up your creative juices and then with pen in hand, draw out a picture and a plan for yourself. You are in control of your own destiny. Your path to achievement will be clearly defined and the trip will shorten considerably when you continue to focus on what inspires you as you continue down that path.

> Procrastination is like a virus: if allowed to take root, its detrimental effect will be widespread in no time.

Take baby steps; don't try to run before you can walk. I know you've heard that many times before but it is something that we have to keep reminding ourselves of. There is a reason why we are told over and over again to take it slowly. If it seems too overwhelming, stop and look at what you are doing… you'll be surprised to see that you're trying to run a 60 yard dash, in record time, while standing in a pool of water. Slow down; take a breath, go back to walking, one step at a time and only in one direction. Take the time you need to complete the task properly… then move on to the next. Every step you take will be an achievement and one step closer to your goal. Not every achievement has to be a big success, it's the series of all your accomplishments put together that will get you there. With every task you complete, you will achieve success.

Life can be busy and it always seems that there are not enough hours in the day to get everything you want done. HOUSE chores: cut the grass, weed the garden, wash the car, paint the bedroom; then there are WORK chores: getting through all the emails, finishing your presentation, working on your website, etc.; and then there are also HOME chores: groceries, cooking, house cleaning, helping with homework, balancing the budget, driving the children to practice, etc.

The one thing that kills any chance of managing all these tasks and having everything work in harmony with effectiveness is procrastination. Procrastination is like a virus, if allowed to take root, its detrimental effect will be widespread in no time. It serves no purpose other than to make life miserable. It is better to tackle the chores and get things done.

I have come across a guideline that I follow that works so well in keeping me on schedule with my tasks; I'd like to share it with you.

To succeed in the completion of any task/project/chore, you need to: Set a deadline. The word, "Deadline" sounds so negative, but really think of this word as a valuable tool. Setting a deadline can decrease stress by motivating you to act. When you think about the chore that needs to get done, and you ignore it, you are causing yourself stress because your choice to not deal with it is weighing heavy on your mind and shoulders. This is a form of stress that you can easily manage if you deal with it.

Once you have a deadline in place, it releases this pressure. Set a deadline and let it inspire you to get started straight away.

Stay on Track. Create a Reminder System. Ok, so now you've set a deadline and it's a great first step. Now don't allow procrastination into the picture by pushing back the deadline you set. The usual culprits to cause you to do this are the "non-fun" tasks. By putting a reminder system (or status update) in place; it gives you accountability. Make a note on your calendar to re-visit the task every 2 weeks or so (you set the schedule), this will serve as a check-in to report to yourself. By asking yourself for a status report at certain intervals, you will ensure that your project keeps moving forward on schedule.

Set a start date. Once you have a project, a deadline, and a plan to stay on track, you can now determine your start date.

Give yourself time to prepare before you jump into the task. By being in control, you will have a better chance to succeed.

Preparation. Gather your tools. Determine what you need and then set up your jobsite. This will give you an environment that is conducive to getting your project finished.

Rest often. Some chores/projects/tasks are more difficult than others. Have you ever been madly working away at something and you don't want to stop to eat or drink or sleep because you are on a roll? Inevitably, you never get the problem solved or the job done because you were too tired or thirsty or overtired. You surrender in the end realizing that it's probably better to leave it and come back the next day. Whether your task is big or small, simple or complicated, easy or difficult, don't defeat yourself by going at it at a crazy pace. This will only frustrate you in the end and put a negative spin on the actual process. Take the time to rest and rejuvenate so that your energy level is always fully charged. This will enable you to successfully complete your task. Managing your chores/tasks/projects in this efficient manner will encourage you to tackle the next with greater enthusiasm.

Much of life is about the process of completing projects in some form or another so, why not learn to make peace with the process. What project has been hanging over your head? What can you do today to free yourself from the bonds of incompletion so you can enjoy more of your precious time?

Achievement is one of life's greatest satisfactions. You deserve to enjoy as much of it as you can. Set yourself a meaningful goal and go after it. Be inspired and you will be inspiration to others. It is a positive force of energy. Begin right now… be committed to your plan so that you can take that dream of yours all the way to the top. You will find that there is a way to make it become a reality and it happened because of the little successes along the way.

Road to Success—Do You Need Directions?

Ah yes, the Road to Success, what a straight stretch of newly paved highway! Not! The Road to Success is anything but and it is never the same road that someone else has necessarily taken either. It's easy to get lost so remember to refer to the proper directions. Keep the positive thoughts in the front of your mind and you will eventually find your way.

The main focus here is to keep going. You can stop to take a rest or to sight-see or to re-energize but then get back on that road and just keep going! The common denominator with every successful person out there is they remained focused on their plan and envisioned where they wanted to be. Realistically, they knew they would most likely have to deal with challenges along the way but with a positive attitude and determination, they saw them as opportunities to fine tune their plan.

When you set your sights on a dream and map out the route to achieve it, make a commitment to yourself to follow through no matter what. Don't lose that feeling of passion that you had when you first decided to go for it. Stay motivated by listening to the success stories of others. You will always find inspiration in their journey. You can and will learn from their experiences. Apply the lessons to learn and grow in your own way.

It is important to remember that there are so many valuable resources available to you. A bookstore is a great place to start. You obviously understand the value of information, after all, you are holding my book in your hands in order to learn something new and for that I am grateful. There are so many success stories that you can learn from. There is a tremendous amount of knowledge in the words you will find in books. Choose a subject that you can identify with. Find an expert in your field. Do you have an idol? Buy a publication that is written well and gives you good insight into their life. Find a mentor. Be a sponge, soak up all the information you can and educate yourself. Let them guide you. With their helpful advice, they can steer you clear of the many pitfalls that they had to encounter. They can even offer shortcuts to help you fast-track your career. Value their expertise and be inspired by them. Take the advice they offer to you and run with it.

Some things will work and seem surprisingly simple and others will most probably seem impossible. They're only temporary hurdles along the way. Just like a long road trip, you must be prepared for the odd flat tire but that can't stop you… all you have to do is fix it in order to move forward and you can get to your destination, right? No big deal. It's an annoyance yes, but not earth shattering in the big picture. Just keep things in proper perspective. Stay focused, stay motivated and be true to yourself.

Through it all, remember to stay positive in all that you do. It will lead you down the road to success. Be positive in your thoughts, in your actions and in your dealings with those around you. Show gratitude for the opportunities you are given in life and your chances to succeed will be returned to you ten-fold. Study that map, stay on course and enjoy the journey!

Be Happy and Live Your Dreams

Do you believe in my message yet? I have been consistent in my delivery throughout this entire book and hopefully by now, you are starting to see the blueprint or pattern I am trying to draw out for you. We are all put here on this earth to experience life, it is a gift. Why not enjoy the ride and experience all that we can? Dream and dream big! Visualize it!

Never think that something is beyond your reach. Don't be surprised when you accomplish something great. Celebrate it and let that propel you forward. Be aware of your thoughts and actions and greet everyday of your life with the attitude of success. Take charge of your life and make your dreams come true.

Thoughts become things, especially when you add positive energy to it. Live each day of your life as the success that you are and the success you want to be. By doing that, you will be creating a formula that will ensure you will achieve greatness. Look at situations as opportunities to grow and learn and improve.

Learn to be happy before your dreams come true. Don't wait until you get to where you want to go or to achieve what you want to do, before you feel happiness. Happiness needs to be an emotion that we allow ourselves to feel. Embrace that emotion. It is a part of life that we must recognize for its benefit to our soul. Let that feeling blossom from your hearts! There will always be things in life that you would love to have; there will always be something that you can strive for. It's the journey that we all must take to greatness. Stay focused on your goals. It is so important to stay happy along the way. Research in positive psychology and neuroscience has shown that the relationship between success and happiness works together but in a specific order. Do not have the belief that you will only be happy when you achieve success, it does not work that way. Happiness is the precursor to success, not the result. Happiness and optimism fuel performance and achievement.

Visualize and use your imagination. As an athlete, visualization was key when doing my final preparation before an event. In my head, I saw myself going through the steps of my program and I focused. My brain knew exactly what

I expected of my body so when the time came to perform physically, everything was in sync. Achieve greatness in your mind, in your dreams and live each day knowing that with goodness and kindness and determination, you can get there. Believe in yourself and just keep moving towards your goal. When you live your life this way, you will be positioning yourself to receive all the good things you are deserving of. Bon Voyage! Enjoy your trip. Our world is filled with abundant opportunities and you will find inspiration everywhere. Be proactive, get motivated and use your positive energy to constantly move yourself onward and upward.

When you are feeling overwhelmed by work, problems, details, bills and worries, help yourself through the stressful situations by making the journey a little more enjoyable. Believe it or not, there is a simple solution to making that happen.

I am inspired by Dr. Maya Angelou, the poet, novelist, educator, civil rights activist. She has said that she learned no matter what happens or how bad something seems, she realizes that life goes on and there will be a tomorrow that will be better. Isn't that how we should all be thinking? It puts things into proper perspective.

Positive Sparkle Tips

Love life, love yourself and love those close to you.

Concentrate on your happiness.

Kindness matters.

Show appreciation and be grateful.

Believe in yourself.

Be passionate about your purpose.

Power through the pain and look at challenges as opportunities to grow and improve.

Today's society seems to focus on the final event, the finished product, the champion and it is merely because it is the most glamorous or sensational part of the journey. What is shown is the medal being awarded, the person being recognized or the latest successful product flying off the shelves. What you are witnessing, via the social media, is a myriad of outstanding achievements and you think that you would love to also experience that level of success but you feel overwhelmed by it all. You have difficulty in comparing yourself to them, thinking that it is not a possibility. I say: Why?

Remember that every Olympian was once a beginner! Every successful person started at ground zero. So why can't you? It does require a plan and a great deal of effort. No one ever sees the hours of grueling work, the trials and errors, the frustration, the pain of the workouts and the failures. (Yes, I said failures.)

Many of the successful athletes, movie and rock stars and business tycoons, over the years, have reached the highest levels of achievement because they indeed failed from time to time. What made these people triumph over others is that they never gave up, in spite of the pitfalls. It is what they did with those situations of failure that turned things around for them. They recognized the importance of learning from their mistakes and to persevere. In doing so, they eventually got it right.

MY ADVICE FOR SUCCESS

Know this... You have the opportunity to be one of the success stories. You can be triumphant at whatever you try. Success is defined in many ways. You determine the value of your own success. To some, it may be defined merely by the salary one earns, the car one drives, or the size of a house one lives in. Success is so much more than that. Success is achievement, whatever the task. Don't base your judgment merely on material things.

Success can be yours if you believe! Whether you are trying to establish yourself in a new environment as a new parent, a new employee, in a new profession, as a business owner or trying to excel as a student and/or as an athlete, you must believe that you will achieve. Starting a business, losing weight, personal development, getting out of debt, these are all things in our daily lives that require the same determination.

It all begins with a dream. Set goals, dream big and be passionate about your purpose. Don't let anyone rain on your parade.

There is no rule book to follow for a personal goal, so it is up to you to seek out available resources to help you on the path.

Ignite your drive with motivation. You must believe in yourself and your abilities! Set your goals and visualize them. They are achievable. You must see success in a new light. It is not just for others to experience, it's available to you too. Believe that.

Be passionate about what matters to you and be true of heart.

Be committed to continue on your path to success. With focus, hard work and determination, anything is possible. Take it one step at a time and be accepting of the lessons.

Be kind in all that you do and with everyone you meet. Kindness matters and you will not only be well respected for being true to your core values but you will have inner peace.

Value your family, your loved ones and the important things in life and be happy.

Live in the moment. The future that we envision can only be realized by living in the present moment. Often, we spend our days waiting for the life that we want to magically appear. It doesn't happen like that in real life. The truth is that your dream life can only become real if you are willing to do the due diligence required to make that vision a reality. This often takes hard work, patience, planning, and the step-by-step execution of your plans in the present moment. Instead of becoming overwhelmed by the vastness of your vision and worrying about whether your future will ever appear, you can focus on what you can do in the present moment so that the future you are dreaming about eventually comes to fruition.

Build the foundation for your dreams today and you will create the tomorrow that you want. You just have to believe!

Don't be afraid of change or challenge. Think of it as

working out. Just like in weight training, with exercise, you strengthen your muscles. There will be some pain but you will grow and improve and get stronger because of it.

Always be grateful and show appreciation. When you feel grateful, the negativity bias automatically releases its grip. Rather than focusing on all the things that are going wrong in your life, remember the many blessings that surround you. When you care about others and feel grateful, you experience renewed love and joy at their presence in your life. Studies have shown that gratitude is linked to decreased envy and materialism.

Give back and help others. The experiences in your life are unique to you and you have gained knowledge because of what you have gone through. Seek out ways to help and empower others with what you have learned.

Believe and trust in your spirituality, whatever your faith. It is where you will find your strength.

Above all else, stay positive. Nurture your positive energy and your spirit and approach life as you were meant to, from the beginning. Your positive energy is a powerful force. When taken care of, it will impact everyone and everything around you. It will attract abundance to you.

These are the elements that feed success. Enjoy each day.

You can win at life, just go out there and be positive, the way you were meant to.

You will sparkle!

Barbara Berezowski and David Porter, World Professional Ice Dance Champions

CAREER HIGHLIGHTS

- PROFESSIONAL ACHIEVEMENTS -

Celebration On Ice
Evening of Champions Gala Performer; Hershey Centre, Toronto, Ontario, Canada; 2006

Legendary Night of Figure Skating
Evening of Champions Gala Performer (celebrating 100 years of Figure Skating in Canada); Air Canada Centre, Toronto, Ontario, Canada; 1999

Stars On Ice
Seoul, South Korea; 1982

Shipstad & Johnson's "Ice Follies"
North America Tour; 1978, 1979, 1980

Toller Cranston's "The Ice Show"
North America Tour; 1976, 1977

Toller Cranston's "The Ice Show"
The Palace Theatre On Broadway; New York, NY, USA; 1978

Guest Appearances on "Stars On Ice"
TV Variety Show; 1976, 1977, 1978, 1979, 1980

World Professional Figure Skating Championships
As Performer and Guest Judge; Jaca, Spain; 1983

World Professional Figure Skating Championships
ICE DANCE CHAMPION; Jaca, Spain; 1977

- AMATEUR ACHIEVEMENTS -

Canadian Winter Olympic Team
Innsbruck, Austria; 1976

World Figure Skating Team
7th Place; Gothenburg, Sweden; 1976

World Figure Skating Team
9th Place; Colorado Springs, CO, USA; 1975

World Figure Skating Team
15th Place; Munich, Germany; 1974

World Figure Skating Team
15th Place; Bratislava, Czechoslovakia; 1973

"Champions On Ice, The World Tour" Member
North America; 1975

Prestige Cutlery Awards Invitational
Ice Dance BRONZE MEDAL; London, England; 1975

Canadian Figure Skating Championship
Ice Dance CHAMPION; London, Ontario, Canada; 1976

Canadian Figure Skating Championship
Ice Dance CHAMPION; Quebec City, Quebec, Canada; 1975

Canadian Figure Skating Championship
Ice Dance SILVER MEDAL; Moncton, New Brunswick, Canada; 1974

Canadian Figure Skating Championship
Ice Dance SILVER MEDAL; Vancouver, British Columbia, Canada; 1973

Canadian Figure Skating Championship
Ice Dance SILVER MEDAL; London, Ontario, Canada; 1972

Canadian Figure Skating Championship
Ice Dance 5th Place; Winnipeg, Manitoba, Canada; 1971

Canadian Figure Skating Championship
Junior Ice Dance CHAMPION; Winnipeg, Manitoba, Canada; 1971

Nouvelles de Moscou International Invitational
Ice Dance 5th Place; Moscow, Russia; 1975

Nouvelles de Moscou International Invitational
Ice Dance 5th Place; Moscow, Russia; 1974

Lake Placid Invitational Figure Skating Championship
Ice Dance CHAMPION; Lake Placid, NY, USA; 1974

Lake Placid Invitational Figure Skating Championship
Ice Dance SILVER MEDAL; Lake Placid, NY, USA; 1973

Skate Canada International Invitational
Ice Dance SILVER MEDAL; Edmonton, Alberta, Canada; 1975

Skate Canada International Invitational
Ice Dance 4th Place; Kitchener, Ontario, Canada; 1974

GOLD Test Level Certified in USA
GOLD Test Level Certified in Canada

- HONORS -

Author
Toronto, Ontario, Canada; February 2013

Etobicoke Sports Hall of Fame, Honored Inductee
Toronto, Ontario, Canada; 1999

Etobicoke Sports Hall of Fame, Founding Board of Governors, Chairperson
Toronto, Ontario, Canada; 1992-1995

"Mom"
Toronto, Ontario, Canada; September 1990
Toronto, Ontario, Canada; January 1989

"Mrs."
Toronto, Ontario, Canada; September 1987

"Miss Canada International"
Finalist; Toronto, Ontario, Canada; 1978

"Miss Olympics"
Innsbruck, Austria 1976

"Miss Canada"
Finalist; Toronto, Ontario, Canada; 1976

"Miss Toronto"
Toronto, Ontario, Canada; 1975-76

"Miss Nouvelles De Moscou"
Moscow, Russia; 1975

"Miss Nouvelles De Moscou"
Moscow, Russia; 1974

"Miss Charm On Ice"
Munich, Germany; 1974

- ACKNOWLEDGEMENTS -

I must give thanks to the people that give me inspiration, encouragement, love and happiness. Some are family and friends and are very near and dear to my heart, others are well known to everyone. They are all on my list because they have given me so much and for that I am so grateful. I want to acknowledge them to show my appreciation. Thank you for your gifts. You all "Sparkle with Positivity!"

My Love and Gratitude to...

My Family

I am so grateful for the years with my husband, the late John Ivan, and for the baseball talent he passed on to our sons. I give thanks for my mom and dad for their unconditional love, support and encouragement. Even though they have both passed on, I think of them everyday. The lessons they taught, I pass on to you... Always be kind, always be passionate, love life and believe in yourself.

My Sons

Brian and Jarrod, you are my loves. I am so blessed to have been given the joy of motherhood. I want you to know that you are with me in every breath I take and every thought I have. I am so proud of what wonderful men you have become… I want you to always follow your dreams with great passion and never give up.

The "Brain Trust"

In a nutshell: you get me. You understand my free spirit and I am so grateful for the fact that you recognize and support my need to spread my wings and fly. I cherish you.

My Big Sister

Terry, what we share is priceless. I am so happy that we have this special bond. Thank you for your love and dedication. You are a wonderful role model. It means more to me than you'll ever know.

My Precious Yorkie, Minnie-Me

You are God's gift to us, sent with unconditional love.

Thank you to the following special people in my life…

Ann and Paul (positively positive and supportive friends), Jacquie (a woman of pure joy and unwavering spirit and deserves so much), Judi (sweet and always there for everyone), my BFF, LeighAnn & Roger (closest friends, tireless fighters of circumstance and yet still so passionate and true), Licia & Jake (very near and dear to my heart), Marijane (my skating coach, my mentor, a graceful Lady), my Mentor, Rick and all my wonderful colleagues at Goodyear Toastmasters, Nadia (for so graciously helping me out with the editing of this book), Monty (for starting me out on this path) and to the very dear family friends that have always been there, no matter what: Blanka, Traudel and Werner, Annie, Ciocia and the Jackowski clan. Always in my thoughts are the dearly departed:

Mary, Theo, Otto, Walter and my Uncle Jack.

A special Thank You to Maxine Taylor, Astrologer, Energy Healer, Spiritual Coach, Teacher, Speaker, Published Author and friend. Maxine SPARKLES! She is a true visionary and an amazing individual and I am proud to call her my friend. She is the author of a wonderful book: *Move Into The Magic,* and I highly recommend you read it. I urge everyone to visit her website at: www.maxinetaylor.com.

Thank you to Dr. Wayne Dyer, Deepak Chopra and Dr. Maya Angelou for your motivation.

And thank you, Denise, Rob and Aaron for assisting with the production of this project. I couldn't have done it without you.

Honorable Mention

Paul Henderson is a man of passionate spirituality and is known throughout the world as Canada's Hockey Legend. (Paul was a member of Team Canada that defeated the Soviet Union in the 1972 Summit Series. He scored the winning goal (known as the goal of the century) in the last 34 seconds of game 7.) I am so grateful to Paul for his special gift of inspiration to me. His kind words of encouragement had a huge impact on me and he has reinforced my belief that with the Lord's guidance, I will continue in this direction in my life with passion and purpose to help others.

Thank you to Scott Hamilton, 1984 Olympic Gold Medalist. Scott is a very generous person of great strength and integrity and is a true Champion in every way.

Thank you to Barb MacDonald of Skate Canada for your support and enthusiasm.

Win At Life and Positively Sparkle!

- ABOUT THE AUTHOR -
BARBARA BEREZOWSKI

Olympian, Author, Hall of Famer
Motivational Speaker
Certified Professional Life Coach

www.winandsparkle.com
www.bberezowski.com

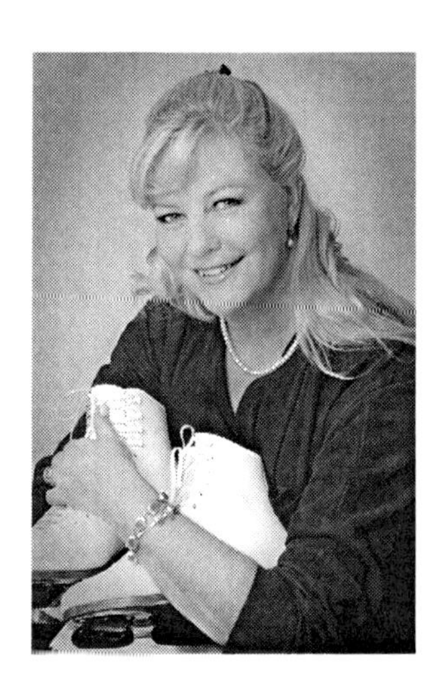

I am a double gold medalist in Canada and the United States and became a world class athlete. I represented Canada and competed in the 1976 Winter Olympic Games in Innsbruck, Austria, a World Professional Figure Skating Champion and a two time Canadian Figure Skating Champion (along with my partner David Porter) in Ice Dance. We went on to perform professionally in skating shows all over North America, Europe and the Far East. Living the life of a celebrity athlete was an exciting time of media attention, spotlights and huge crowds of adoring fans. Along with my devotion to skating,

I have always been open to experiencing new and different things. I was also Miss Toronto, a Miss Canada Finalist, Miss Charm On Ice (Munich, Germany), twice named Miss Moscow (at a skating event in Russia) and voted Miss Olympics (Innsbruck, Austria). Looking back on all that now, I am convinced those honors were a direct result of my positive energy.

In fact, there have been many situations throughout my life where I can say the same. Every life experience I've had has led me to where I am today. It has always been important to me to inspire and motivate, this passion has now guided me to become a Certified Professional Life Coach and a Motivational Speaker. I have my mother to thank for giving me courage and my father for teaching me the importance of nurturing my inner strength and my positive energy. Like him, I love life, I live with a positive outlook and I choose to lead by example. This is especially true when raising my two wonderful sons, Brian and Jarrod. Above all else, they are my true happiness.

"Be passionate. Love life. Believe in yourself."
Barbara Berezowski

"People are like stained-glass windows. They sparkle and shine when the sun is out, but when the darkness sets in; their true beauty is revealed only if there is a light from within."
Elizabeth Kubler-Ross
(Swiss-American psychiatrist and author)

A pair of skates is all it takes...
Learn to skate with SKATE CANADA.

SKATE CANADA is the largest figure skating governing body in the world. They provide standards and rules for the figure skating activities of their members. The Association qualifies and appoints judges, referees and other officials, conducts training seminars for skaters and coaches, provides financial support to national team athletes and disseminates information concerning figure skating to the general public.

Skate Canada also promotes the National Coaching Certification Program and organizes free skating and synchronized team skating competitions and the annual Skate Canada International. From time to time, Skate Canada also hosts selected ISU skating events.

Go to skatecanada.ca for more information.

For more inspiration
and
information on how to book
Barbara Berezowski
to speak at your next event,
please visit
www.winandsparkle.com
www.bberezowski.com

CPSIA information can be obtained at www.ICGtesting.com
Printed in the USA
LVOW13063405031З

322647LV00001B/21/P

9 780991 778409